£7.99

658.4093

CAU

THE SUNDAY TIMES

Moreton Morrell Site

Organise
Yourself

John Caunt

Moreton Morrell Site

 KOGAN PAGE | *CREATING SUCCESS*

First published 2000
Reprinted 2002, 2003

Kogan Page Limited
120 Pentonville Road
London N1 9JN

www.kogan-page.co.uk

© John Caunt, 2000

British Library Cataloguing in Publication Data

A CIP record for this book is available from the British Library.

ISBN 0 7494 3261 6

Typeset by Jean Cussons Typesetting, Diss, Norfolk
Printed and bound in Great Britain by Clays Ltd, St Ives plc

contents

introduction

The working environment of today is characterized by constantly rising pressure to deliver with fewer resources. Against a background of restructuring and cost-cutting we are expected to keep a larger number of balls in the air and to do so with less support. In many areas of work, secretarial support and clerical assistance which would have been the norm 10 years ago can no longer be taken for granted. The picture is increasingly one of direct phone lines, desktop PCs, e-mail communication and self-sufficient professionals responsible for their own personal organization. The information age provides us with some of the tools to organize our working lives, but it also presents us with many new challenges in the form of additional paperwork, expectations of immediacy, and interruptions to our routines.

To cope with all of this we need to be organized. We need to handle time, people, paper and technology as efficiently and effectively as possible in order to deliver the results on which we will be judged. Being organized means:

- less time spent firefighting and responding to crises;
- sharper focus on the things that matter most in terms of producing results;
- the ability to see your way through complex problems and challenges;

- more time for family, friends and leisure;
- reduced stress and fatigue;
- enhanced reputation for competence;
- greater sense of achievement;
- the chance to step back and take pride in a job well done.

Even though the benefits of greater organization are clear, we present ourselves with excuses for failing to acquire them:

Excuse 1 – 'The ability to be organized is something innate. It's a quality that you either possess or lack, and I just don't have it.'

Certainly it's true that we vary in our natural tendency towards being organized, but it isn't true that there is nothing we can do to overcome that inclination. Studies of brain function have revealed differences in the way that the two hemispheres of the brain operate. Work by American psychologist Jerre Levy and others demonstrated that the left hemisphere is superior in analytical functioning, while the right hemisphere is superior in many forms of visual and spatial performance and tends to be more holistic in its functioning than the left. It has been shown that, although we use both hemispheres of the brain simultaneously, there is a tendency in most of us to favour one side or the other. We are either left-brain dominant or right-brain dominant. In simple terms, the left-brain dominant person tends towards an organized, analytical and methodical approach while right-brain dominant types tend to be more creative and intuitive. However, just because we may favour one way of operating, it does not mean that we are unable to develop the skills associated with the other hemisphere. In truth, we all display skills associated with both sides of the brain. When it comes to organizing skills, the right-brain dominant person may just have to work a bit harder at it than the left-brain dominant individual. And just in case you are wondering, I'll own up now to being a person who has had to work quite hard at becoming organized.

Excuse 2 – 'There is no way that I could be organized in this place. The constant interruptions, the crises, the disorganized colleagues.'

Yes, there are plenty of workplaces where it is hard to be organized, but that is no reason to give up. In the chapters that follow we will look at how you can take control of your working environment and reduce interruptions and distractions. We will look at the effect of good planning in forestalling crises, effective delegation which minimizes colleague dependency, and ways of helping others to be more organized.

Excuse 3 – 'I would like to be more organized but I'm just too busy to spend time on it at the moment. Perhaps in a couple of months' time.'

In today's work climate, the person who postpones action in the hope of having more time a month, two months, six months from now, is destined to be forever disappointed. And what does 'being too busy' really mean? It is possible to spend your working days scurrying in every direction and achieving little – you may be busy but not effective. Targeted activity is what brings results, and improved organization is largely about targeting your activity. The time commitment to improving your personal organization does not have to be that great. It requires some commitment and consistency of purpose over several weeks, but the time-saving benefits accrue quickly, so any time invested now will be rapidly rewarded.

We all have our organizational strengths and weaknesses, so before launching into the first chapter, take a moment to ask yourself where your particular shortcomings lie. It will help you to focus on those parts of the book which have the greatest significance for you, and thus maximize the investment of your time.

personal organization checklist

Which of the following statements apply to you?

1. There is a lack of overall direction to my work.
2. I have difficulty extracting priorities from the mass of tasks and issues that come my way.
3. My working day seems to slip away with little achieved.
4. I don't plan my time adequately.
5. I end the day with more items on my 'to do' list than I started with.
6. I find it hard to estimate how long some tasks are going to take.
7. Deadlines seem to creep up on me.
8. I'm not sure that I make best use of the times when my energy levels are highest.
9. I flit in and out of routine tasks, often letting them interrupt more important work.
10. I tend to postpone tasks I don't like.
11. Trivial tasks assume greater importance than they should.
12. I sometimes have difficulty knowing where to start on complex tasks and projects.
13. I would like to be more systematic in my decision making.
14. The volume of incoming paperwork is a problem for me.
15. I don't often tackle paperwork when I first look at it.
16. I am often unable to decide what to do with documents I receive.
17. I would like to assimilate documents more quickly.
18. I forget a lot of what I read.
19. I find myself attending too many unproductive meetings.
20. I don't think I delegate enough.

21. Colleagues bombard me with information I don't need.
22. I am plagued by interruptions
23. Too often I take on tasks I should refuse.
24. My office layout isn't conducive to good organization.
25. There are piles of paper in my office, my desktop is cluttered, cupboards and drawers are crammed.
26. I spend a lot of time looking for things.
27. My files are disorganized.
28. I am concerned that I am not adequately utilizing technology to organize my work.
29. I don't use the Internet as effectively as I might.
30. I would like to be more organized when I am away from the office.

This book does not aim at any particular occupational group or echelon of management. The pressures of the modern workplace are fairly universal, and the steps to improved personal organization are pretty much the same whatever your level in the organization you work for. There will be differences, of course, in the amount of support you are able to call upon, and the number of others you are responsible for. But whether you are a new entrant, an aspiring or recently appointed supervisor, an established manager in a private enterprise or public undertaking, or a self-employed professional, there is something here for you.

In those sections that deal with aspects of new technology, it is assumed that most readers will have some awareness of computers, but that it may be very limited or piecemeal. Where specific techniques are referred to, I have used as examples the most popular applications at the time of writing. In particular this applies to the Windows 95/98 operating system, Microsoft Internet Explorer, and Outlook Express e-mail software. Users of other applications and operating systems may need to refer to their software documentation or help file.

know where you are going

When you are being bombarded every day with a multiplicity of tasks, other people's priorities, distractions and interruptions, it's all too easy to take your eye off the ball. You need to keep yourself on track by an ability to separate the important from the trivial. The first step to being organized occurs not in your in tray, your filing cabinet or your computer, but in your head. If you are to take control of your working life and begin to make a difference, you must first make sure that you have a clear understanding of your role and primary objectives.

a clear understanding of your role

In a rapidly changing work environment, this can be harder than it seems. In all probability you have a job description tucked away somewhere from the time that you were appointed. Have you looked at it recently, and if so did it tell you anything? Unfortunately, job descriptions are often written in rather vague terms, and tend to become quickly out of date as roles shift to meet new requirements.

If you have no job description, or it isn't helpful, can you sum up as briefly as possible what your job is about – the key functions that you perform for the organization you work for? And do you have a set of primary objectives that can give direction to your work and measure your performance? Ideally such objectives should be set firmly in the context of the organization you are working for. An effective organization will be one that sets clear corporate aims and objectives which are cascaded through departmental plans and down to individual objectives agreed between you and your boss. But the ideal can be elusive. If you are able to answer yes to all the following, you're off to a good start:

- ▨ Does the organization you work for have stated objectives that make sense to you?
- ▨ Are they reflected in coherent goals for that part of the organization in which you work?
- ▨ Do you have clear objectives that you have agreed with your boss?
- ▨ From these, are you able to establish your priorities over the next three months/six months/year?

There may be various reasons why you can't answer all these questions positively. The organization you work for may be confused about its purpose and direction. Its culture may not favour open communication, or it may be going through a time of rapid change with resultant ambiguity and conflicts over roles and priorities. You may work for a boss whose greatest strengths do not include clear and negotiated objective setting, or worse, you may be responsible to more than one boss, each of whom has a different set of priorities.

At the end of the day, there is only so much that you can do about others' lack of clarity. If you are unsure about corporate or departmental objectives, you may be able to seek clarification from your boss, or gain a greater understanding by reading public documents like annual reports. If your boss is the sort who is not very good at setting and agreeing objectives with you, then you might consider structuring what you think should be your objectives and asking your boss to confirm or amend them. Take care not to respond to vagueness further up the line by simply going your own way. You may have to formulate your objectives and priorities unaided, but make sure that you share them with your boss and obtain agreement to them.

In the context of personal organization, it is also important to think beyond just your primary work role. You may also want to set objectives in respect of your personal and career development, or your life outside work. You might, for example, decide that one of your aims from greater organization is to free yourself from the habit of taking work home at weekends, and thereby to spend more time with your children, take up a new sport or hobby, and get away for weekend breaks.

setting objectives

Whether or not you find yourself setting overall objectives for your role, you will need to engage in some objective setting to help your detailed planning and organization. You will want to break down overall objectives into smaller units of achievement and to define objectives for projects you undertake. There may also be others working for you with whom you need to determine and agree objectives. Unfortunately, objective setting is often hedged around with a certain amount of jargon and mystique that can deter the uninitiated. But it doesn't have to be a big deal. An objective is just a tool, the purpose of which is to transform amorphous challenges into things you can get your teeth into. Like any tool, you need to be able to work with it. It should be meaningful to you and anyone else to whom it refers. It needs to be clear and precise, but don't go overboard in your search for complete precision. An objective which is a little loose is better than no objective at all. This is particularly the case when you are setting objectives for yourself rather than for others. You know what you mean, others might not. Take care also not to set too many objectives. The more you have, the more difficult it is to focus on what needs to be done. Try to produce objectives that are SMART – specific, measurable, achievable, result-oriented and time-related.

specific

The more general an objective, the harder it is to focus on those tasks and activities necessary to bring about its achievement.

measurable

Without a measurable element to your objectives you won't know whether you have achieved them. If, for example, I set out an objective aimed at reducing customer complaints, it wouldn't have much meaning without a quantity being mentioned. Would a reduction of one be enough to meet the objective? However, don't engage in quantification for the sake of it. Figures plucked out of the air tend not to be helpful.

achievable

Any objective you set should be achievable. The reason? You are using the objective as a way of getting things done and obtaining the reinforcement that comes from success. It is not the purpose of objectives to add unnecessary stress to your life and deliver the negative reinforcement of failure. So set your objectives with an element of challenge, but make sure that they are not out of reach.

result-oriented

Objectives should be described in terms of results delivered rather than activities. If, as part of my drive to become more organized, I determine that I will arrive at work an hour earlier in the mornings, this simply describes the activity. I can spend that hour drinking coffee and chatting, and I will still achieve the objective.

time-related

Objectives need a clear deadline by which they will be completed. This links closely with the requirement that they be achievable. An objective may be achievable in one timescale but not in another.

---

activity

Can you identify between five and eight key objectives that currently apply to your role? Try writing them down, taking account of the above principles.

Having clear objectives is the starting point for a more organized way of working. From them you need to identify the tasks which will lead you to their achievement, and to set about incorporating those tasks into your schedule. We will look at this process in Chapter 2 in conjunction with time management. But first, let's consider three further aspects to knowing where you are going.

seeing the big picture and the small picture

Just focusing on long-range objectives can be discouraging. It's like climbing a mountain. As you labour through the foothills, you can see the summit ahead of you all the time, but progress towards it seems painfully slow. It is very important to maintain a sense of achievement along the way. You can get that by providing yourself with milestones – breaking down major objectives into smaller steps and giving yourself credit for achieving them.

balancing the different elements in your job

Your job is made up of a whole variety of elements, each competing for your time and attention. In a complex role it's easy to be sidetracked into one element to the detriment of others. A particular project may start to take up more of your attention than anticipated, or an interesting issue may draw you away from other priorities. It's another dimension to the big picture. You need to apportion your limited resources in a balanced way to ensure that you make progress towards all your objectives.

Roger Willis is the personnel manager of an organization employing 500 people. His responsibilities cover the full gamut of the personnel function – human resource planning, appointment, induction and training, staff welfare, personnel policies and procedures etc. He is at pains to present the personnel department as caring and accessible, perceiving these qualities as lacking in some other parts of the organization.

Consequently he spends a large part of his time engaged in one-to-one counselling of employees and acting as a mediator in disputes. He likes this part of his job and is good at it, but the outcome is that more and more people beat a path to his door, and line managers refer individual problems to him. Aspects of his primary role, such as ensuring that there are clear personnel policies and that people are appropriately trained for their jobs, get lower priority because he is constantly responding to individual problems.

Whatever your job, there is likely to be a range of conflicting demands upon your time. So take a few moments to consider adjustments you might make now to the elements that make up your workload. Ask yourself:

1. Are there elements of my job that are currently taking a greater proportion of my time and attention than they should? If so, what are they?
2. Why have they become excessively demanding?
3. What elements of my role should I be spending more time on?
4. What might I do to start adjusting the balance between these?

determining day-to-day priorities

Life would be easy if, having planned the way forward, we could quietly and systematically pursue the achievement of our objectives. But it's seldom like that. In all probability, your working day is spent responding to a multitude of routine chores, crises, requests and interruptions. In the face of this bombardment, you need a means of determining which tasks will take priority. A simple way of looking at this is to define every demand upon your time, whether it is self-generated or comes in the form of a request, in terms of its importance and its urgency.

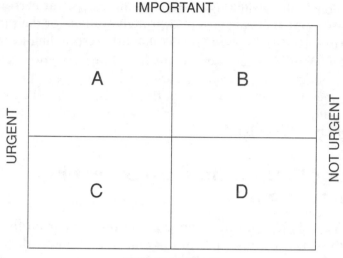

IMPORTANT

A	B
C	D

URGENT

NOT URGENT

UNIMPORTANT

Figure 1.1   *Determining priorities*

Any task can be slotted into one of the four sectors in Figure 1.1.

sector A: tasks that are important and urgent

Items that are both important and urgent are the ones to which you should give immediate attention. They are the 'tackle first' items in your schedule. It's worth asking, however, whether better planning could have made them less urgent.

sector B: tasks that are important but not urgent

These are items which must not be ignored. They are often concerned with longer-term objectives and you need to ensure that you find the time to progress them. Dealing with them is part of seeing the big picture. The greatest source of conflicting priorities tends to occur between this category and those items in category C. Given inadequate attention, category B tasks may suddenly be promoted to extreme category A when a deadline looms. Plan your time effectively to reduce this possibility, and try to ensure that as much of your time as possible is spent on category B tasks.

sector C: tasks that are urgent but unimportant

Don't let these items draw your attention away from those in group B. Just because they are urgent doesn't make them any more important. Question why they are urgent. Often you will find it is no more than a gloss applied by somebody else to justify their existence or cover their inefficiency. They may be tasks to delegate or to quietly run into the sand. Of course, your decision on what to do about them will need to be guided by the politics of your workplace. If your boss is the one asking, and regards the task as important and urgent, then some adjustment of your own assessment may be necessary.

sector D: tasks that are neither important nor urgent

You should not be wasting your time and energy on these. Frequently, tasks in this category are used as self-generated distractions – excuses for not getting down to other more important work which is viewed with some degree of apprehension. Recognize them for what they are and focus your efforts on tasks in the other sectors.

the 80:20 rule

The 80:20 rule was originated by an Italian economist – Vilfredo Pareto – around 1900. He discovered a consistent phenomenon that about 80 per cent of the wealth of countries was controlled by around 20 per cent of the people. This 80:20 principle has since been expanded to include all aspects of business, and has been particularly applied to elements of management – notably '80 per cent of the results come from 20 per cent of the effort'. The accuracy of this relationship may be disputed, but the fact remains that by concentrating your effort into the important few actions rather than the trivial many, you are liable to achieve more impressive results.

summary

The first steps towards better organization consist of:

- establishing a clear understanding of your role;
- setting precise objectives;
- viewing the big picture and the small picture;
- balancing the different elements of your job;
- determining day-to-day priorities.

organize your time

Time is unlike most other resources in that it is shared out equally. We all have the same amount of it each day. The differences between us lie in how we choose to spend it and how far we try to stretch it.

Your aim in managing your time better is either to reduce the number of hours you spend at work, or to achieve more in the same number of hours. It is a matter of ordering priorities. When you say, 'I just haven't got the time for this', you are really saying, 'Something else is more important to me than this'. The problem is that, through inadequate planning and monitoring, we lose control of our schedule and fail to distinguish between the high pay-off and low pay-off demands on our time. We find ourselves saying, 'I haven't time for this' to an important commitment because we have already spent too much of it on trivia.

In this chapter, then, we will look at techniques for planning and tracking the tasks that we need to spend time on. First, however, let's consider how you currently spend your time.

how you use time now

It is useful, before embarking on a new planning regime for your time, to give some attention to how you are currently spending it. Some time management programmes propose that you maintain a rigid time log for a couple of weeks. I don't see this as necessary, but I do suggest that you carry out a simple monitoring exercise over a period of several days.

monitoring exercise – task importance

The purpose of this exercise is to heighten your awareness of the relative importance of the tasks which go to make up your day, and to signal those areas on which you may concentrate your efforts for improvement. On a blank sheet of A4, recreate the diagram we encountered in Chapter 1, and label the four sectors as shown in Figure 2.1.

A. important and urgent	B. important, not urgent
C. urgent, not important	D. neither urgent nor important

Figure 2.1 *Monitoring your tasks*

Keep the sheet to hand throughout your working day and note the tasks you carry out in the appropriate sector as indicated in the example in Figure 2.2.

A. important and urgent	B. important, not urgent
Finished presentation for tomorrow's board meeting. Implemented emergency payment arrangements following payroll computer crash.	Produced plan for office relocation. Reviewed progress with team. Investigated possible new business lead.
C. urgent, not important	D. neither urgent nor important
Responded to interruptions. Wrote replies to routine correspondence which could have been delegated.	Sat for 2 hours in irrelevant meeting I could have avoided. Browsed junk mail. Found some minor tasks to avoid less pleasant work.

Figure 2.2 *Examples of priorities*

Complete a sheet each day for a minimum of three days and compare them, asking yourself the following questions:

- ■ Did I have any difficulty in distinguishing between those tasks that are important and those that are unimportant? If so, what steps do I need to take to remove this confusion?
- ■ Roughly what proportion of my time is currently being spent on unimportant tasks? (Sectors C and D)
- ■ What could I do to reduce the number of tasks appearing in these sectors?
- ■ Was enough of my time spent on tasks in Sector B?
- ■ How can I increase time devoted to these tasks?

If, in the course of this exercise, you find yourself discarding or delegating tasks you would normally have carried out, that's fine. It's the start of organizing your time better. As an alternative to completing the sheets as you work, you may prefer to fill them in retrospectively, looking back over what you have done in the last week.

planning and tracking your time

Having examined how your time is currently being spent, the next step is to adopt a workable system for planning and tracking your time through the days, weeks and months ahead.

planning

You need to be able to:

- determine your objectives;
- identify the steps needed to achieve your objectives;
- break projects and assignments down into their component tasks;
- decide how long you expect activities to take;
- decide when you will need to complete tasks over the coming days and weeks;
- identify what you will need from others in order that you can complete your own tasks.

tracking

You need to be able to keep track of:

- your contacts;
- your meetings and appointments;
- what you have done and what remains to be done;

■ who is doing what for you and by when;
■ when you need to follow up contacts and leads.

planning your time

In line with what has already been said about viewing the big picture and the small picture, you need to be able to plan over different time frames. The relative importance of longer-term and short-term planning will vary according to the nature of your work, but you may like to look at planning over three time frames. The first, and most general, might be an overall view of the next three months in terms of major development activities; the second, a week-by-week view to be sure that you are able to fit in the necessary preparation for impending commitments and deadlines; and the third, a detailed daily plan to ensure that you achieve a balance between important and urgent items and tasks which contribute towards longer-term objectives.

It sounds complicated, but it doesn't need to be. The more detailed views sit inside the more general like Russian dolls. If planning your time is not one of your current strengths, you may want to start by looking at it on a daily basis, but within a week or so you should aim to embrace all three time perspectives.

planning your day

The time to plan your day is not first thing in the morning, but at the end of the previous working day. Once you get into the habit it will take no more than a few minutes before you pack up for the day. The task is completed while your brain is still in work mode and the following morning you are spared any indecisiveness and time-wasting while you gear yourself up for the day. You know exactly what you are aiming to do and you are able to hit the ground running. Resist the temptation to be overambitious in the number of tasks you set yourself, and don't book yourself up so heavily that there is no space for the unexpected. You may find it useful to allocate a priority to tasks: A, B and C or 'must be done today', 'should be done today' and 'it would be nice to do if time permits'. Crossing completed items off your list is very satisfying and helps to keep you on track, but resist the temptation to include too many easy hits on your list – small tasks which are there simply to be crossed off.

mapping out your week

Just like daily planning, the time to map out your week is at the end of the previous week. You're not concerned with the same level of detail as for the daily plan, but you are aiming to establish an overall balance to your week, and to ensure that you are not caught on the hop. You will be thinking about what information you need to ask for on Monday in order that it is available for a task that must be completed by Friday; what you will have to do on Tuesday to prepare for that meeting on Wednesday; how much you will need to do each day to carry forward a major long-term initiative.

A regular Friday afternoon session when you map out the coming week is also a good time to review your work in the current week and give yourself credit for the things you have achieved. Don't succumb to frustration about the tasks you have not managed to complete – you will rarely achieve everything you aim for – re-evaluate your plans and move on.

overviewing the next three months

This is at a different level again from your weekly planning. It's about major blocks of time that will need to be devoted to projects and development tasks. The aim here is to ensure that deadlines in respect of different assignments don't clash, and that the timescales you allocate to major tasks are realistic. You are most likely to engage in this sort of activity in conjunction with planning a particular project. We will examine project planning in a little more detail at the end of this chapter.

tracking your time

Tracking is about keeping on top of the activities you have planned – ensuring that you are reminded when actions are due, and monitoring your progress towards achievement of the objectives you have set yourself. The key to this is simplicity. Wherever possible, avoid recording information in multiple locations. Using a desk diary in the office and a pocket diary when you are at meetings and on the road is a recipe for over-looked commitments. If it is essential to have information in different formats, make sure that there is one master record. Limit the amount of manual transfer of information as far as possible to avoid oversights and minimize wasted effort.

planning and tracking tools

The tools you can use to assist you may range from a blank sheet of paper to a palmtop computer. There is no one 'best' way of working. Choose tools that fit your preferred personal style and the nature of your work. It is important to realize that a poorly used tool can impede rather than improve your effec-tiveness.

'to do' lists

For all the technology that has swept into personal information management over recent years, the simple paper-based 'to do' list is still the most widely used tool. The issue, of course, is where is the list generated from? It isn't a lot of use if it is just composed of a collection of items that pop into your head each morning. Some time management programmes propose a master list consisting of everything you need to do, from which you will extract those items that relate to a particular day or week as appropriate. A 'to do' list also needs to be closely inte-grated with your meetings and appointments. A daily list of things to do which fails to take account of the other activity which makes up your day is clearly not achieving its purpose.

paper-based planners and organizers

In the 1980s no self-respecting manager would be seen without a leather-bound personal organizer, and a visit to an office stationery supplier today will reveal that there are still plenty around, produced in a wide range of styles and prices. The basic format is a small ring binder with indexed sections containing pre-printed insert pages. Typical inserts available include:

- year planners;
- diaries in various formats;
- daily planning sheets – appointments and things to do;
- monthly objectives and project planning sheets;
- telephone and address book inserts;
- pages for notes;
- budget planning and expenses planning.

The idea is that all necessary working information is contained in one convenient folder. Users can switch their attention easily from a long-term to a short-term view and can swiftly update information wherever they might be. New pages can be inserted and redundant ones removed so that the organizer remains indefinitely expandable and always up to date. The downside is that there may be some need to transfer information from one page to another and some of the tools, year planners for example, are a little too small for serious use. Also, if you have a large number of contacts for your address book or need to make a lot of notes, you can find these sections becoming unwieldy. The great advantage of paper-based organizers is that you can take them anywhere, and they don't beep at you in meetings.

PC-based personal information managers (PIMs)

These are, in effect, customized databases for storing and tracking personal information. There are a number of well-known commercial packages such as: Lotus Organizer, Starfish

Sidekick, Microsoft Schedule Plus and Microsoft Outlook (NB I am referring here to the full commercial version of Microsoft Outlook rather than Outlook Express which comes free with Internet Explorer and has only limited PIM facilities). A personal information manager is generally included with the major integrated office suites, and there are dozens of good examples which can be downloaded from the Internet, some free of charge. An example is given in Figure 2.3. Typical contents are:

▦ an address book to manage contacts;
▦ an appointments scheduler, which may be integrated with the address book or with a monthly or annual time planner, and which offers a reminder facility;
▦ 'to do' lists which can be arranged under subject headings and may permit some simple project planning and tracking in terms of target date, person responsible, planned duration and percentage of the task completed;
▦ recording of time spent on activities and expenses tracking;
▦ free note space which may be adapted to particular purposes, and generally allows importation of information from other packages.

The great benefit of a PIM is the way that information can be integrated and viewed in different ways, without the hassle of manually transferring it. You can plan your activities within a project, and slot tasks into your schedule over a period of weeks, taking full account of your other commitments. At the appointed time, the 'to dos' will pop up in the diary section of your PIM and won't go away until you have signalled them as complete. Regularly recurring commitments need to be entered only once. You can view the big picture and the small with a click of the mouse and link people in the address book to assignments and appointments. Routine reference information

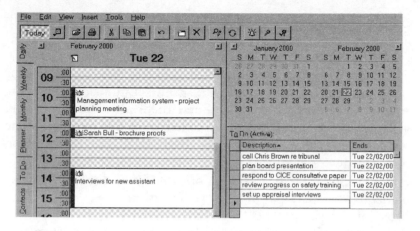

Figure 2.3 *PIM software – daily appointments and 'to do' list (Microsoft Schedule Plus)*

or essential notes are easily incorporated, and it is simple to track time and cost . The downside is that you need a computer to hand in order to access all these facilities. To some extent this drawback is overcome by the use of a pocket organizer or personal digital assistant.

The full version of Microsoft Outlook provides integration of e-mail management and PIM and has a number of extremely useful features. It allows the sharing of diary information over the Internet or an internal company network, and includes an 'autopick' feature which can greatly assist in the scheduling of meetings by identifying the times when attendees are free and facilities available. This assumes, of course, that everybody concerned has taken the trouble to keep their personal schedules updated – not something you can necessarily rely upon! It is also easy to generate status reports on tasks contained within the 'to do' section of Outlook and send them via e-mail to a predetermined distribution list.

pocket organizers and personal digital assistants (PDAs)

These hardware devices range from simple electronic address books to full-blown hand-held PCs. In the mid-range you will get most of the features of a PIM software package (address book, calendar, scheduler, reminder, notes) in an easily pocketable device. At the high end, you will also get cut-down versions of standard word-processing and spreadsheet software, together with e-mail and Internet access. As with all computer hardware, performance becomes ever more impressive at ever reducing cost. If you have previously dismissed PDAs as inadequate, it may pay to look again at more recent models. Most of the smaller PDAs are menu-driven or touch-screen devices and may incorporate handwriting recognition. They are not intended for large-scale data input, and even those hand-held PCs with proper keyboards are generally small and fiddly. However, full-sized folding keyboards are now optional accessories for some machines. Their great strength is portability. If you are running time management software on your desktop PC, it is essential that you are easily able to synchronize its data with that in your pocket computer. Entering the same data separately into two computers is to be avoided at all costs – a recipe for total chaos. Facilities for data synchronization have greatly improved over recent years, but make sure before buying that there are no hardware or software incompatibilities between your choice of PDA and your main machine.

which system is the best?

It all depends on the way you like to work. Paper-based systems are less powerful in terms of cross-referencing, and require a degree of duplication. Inputting or extracting information from computer-based systems can interrupt the flow of other activities.

It is possible to operate a compromise solution which is in part paper, part electronic. It is less efficient than a wholly electronic system, but enjoys the flexibility of paper. A number of PIMs will print out pages in the format used by standard paper-based organizers. I have worked with a combined computer and paper system for a number of years. I put it forward as just one way of working and certainly not *the* way, and I will freely admit that it is a way of working established when PDAs were not as powerful as they are now.

I use a computerized personal information manager to plan and track tasks, but I don't like to keep my computer on all the time or carry a PDA everywhere, so I routinely transfer information to paper. I feed appointments and things 'to do' into the PIM, with dates by which they need to be achieved and priorities. The software will remind me when a deadline approaches and will carry on reminding me until I indicate that the task has been completed. I like the fact that I can enter initial ideas, subsequently build them up into projects and then schedule the activities that need to be completed over weeks or months.

But in the hustle of a working day I prefer to scribble a note rather than make an entry in the computer, so I always have a standard notebook with me. Into it go notes of interviews and meetings, outcomes of discussions and telephone conversations, commitments, contacts and ideas. At the end of each day I will go through the day's jottings and enter any aspect of these which has relevance for future activity into my PIM. I mark the start and finish date of every notebook on the outside cover, and keep them as a permanent record I can refer to if ever I need more background on an issue.

Also at the end of each day, I examine the following day's appointments and tasks 'to do'. It takes just a few minutes, and allows me to remind myself about priorities and assess the amount of time I expect each task to take. Depending on the pressure of the day, I may be able to schedule time for additional tasks from an undated 'to do' list or complete parts of more major tasks. I print out the schedule, and the following day I cross off the tasks as they are completed. They will be signalled as done in my PIM at the end of the day, at the same time that I plan the next day's tasks. Any that I haven't managed to get to are automatically carried over to the following day.

---

activity

Before leaving this section, take a few moments to reflect on how you currently plan and track your time. What changes might you usefully make to the tools you are using at present?

---

scheduling your time – estimating time requirements

You start the day with, let's say, a dozen items on your 'to do' list. What confidence do you have that at the end of the day they will all have been crossed off? Not a great deal unless you have made some estimate of how long each task is likely to take, and fitted them in with the other commitments that make up your day. It isn't just about the confidence and credibility boost that comes from achieving what you set out to do, although that should not be underestimated. Estimating time requirements of tasks allows you to use the available slots in your day appropriately. If you have half an hour between commitments, you want, wherever possible, to fill it with a half-hour task. Discovering that a task you thought was going to take half an hour is really going to take an hour may result in additional time spent refocusing your attention when you eventually come back to it.

You will never achieve time estimation perfection. Tasks will contain unforeseen elements, and we all have a tendency to overestimate the time taken to complete those tasks we dislike, and to underestimate the ones we like. But taking a moment to think about what is involved with a task before you pop it into your schedule can greatly help the management of your working day.

slotting tasks into the day

Your day is likely to be made up of fixed commitments – appointments and meetings – and flexible ones – the tasks on your 'to do' list. Having roughly estimated the time you expect these tasks to take, you can then get an idea of when you will hope to fit them in. Don't seek to rigidly plan your whole day in advance, and don't spend a lot of time on the process. It should be a quick and simple way of giving your day shape and balance, fitting tasks into appropriate time slots, not a bureaucratic exercise. Half-hour time slots are a manageable way of dividing up your day, although for some smaller tasks you may want to think in terms of quarter-hour slots. Group several minor tasks – five or six phone calls for example – into a half-hour slot. Allow a bit of padding in your time estimates for some of the inevitable calls and interruptions. There is a great satisfaction boost to be had from completing a task in less than the time you expected it to take, but you also need to maintain your cool when tasks are taking longer than planned. Above all, stay flexible and deal with whatever the day throws at you.

activity – improving your scheduling accuracy

If it isn't your current practice to estimate the time that tasks will occupy, start by setting a rough estimate alongside each item in your 'to do' list. Once you are under way, monitor the accuracy of your time planning for several days:

- Give a rough time estimate to every task on your 'to do' list.
- When you complete the task, enter the actual time taken alongside the estimate.
- Compare the differences over the period of a week.

- Are there any patterns of consistent over- or underestimation?
- Are there reasons you can discern for the inaccuracy?
- What can you do to improve accuracy?

procrastination

Some element of postponement is both inevitable and necessary in a busy work schedule, but we give ourselves needless stress and reduce our effectiveness if we indulge in habitual procrastination, the biggest time-waster. We present ourselves with excuses such as:

- 'I haven't got all the information I need to tackle this job.'
- 'I don't have time at the moment to do it justice.'
- 'There are other deadlines which are more pressing.'
- 'If I do nothing with this, it will probably go away.'

We tackle the easier items and those which may be superficially more attractive while some of the most important tasks remain undone. But the stress of not tackling a particular task is often greater than that involved in carrying it out. We waste time and energy worrying about the things we have not done when, with a little more resolve, they could be consigned to the out tray. The reasons for procrastination include:

- fear of failing or making a mistake;
- boredom;
- uncertainty over how to go about a task;
- anxiety about the possible consequences of your action;
- perfectionism – unwillingness to start a task unless it can be completed perfectly.

Putting tasks off to another day is not the only problem. Just as prevalent is the tendency to delay getting down to the main job in hand by using minor tasks as self-imposed diversions. This is very time-consuming and energy-destructive. With a little self-discipline it can be overcome.

strategies for beating procrastination

- ▓ Own up to it. Recognizing that the problem exists is the first step to overcoming it.
- ▓ Identify the real reason why you are postponing the task.
- ▓ Discriminate between the routine and the difficult tasks and give the latter priority on your 'to do' lists.
- ▓ Schedule times in your diary for tackling tasks you don't like.
- ▓ Tackle boredom by allowing yourself short controlled breaks, but don't give up on the designated time slot for tackling a difficult task.
- ▓ Note the frequency with which tasks you have been avoiding turn out less fearsome than expected. Use this knowledge as a reference to help overcome future anxieties.
- ▓ Recognize when the resources at your disposal are sufficient to achieve a good job. Don't strive after perfection.
- ▓ Reward yourself for successfully dealing with difficult tasks.
- ▓ Look for an easy point of entry to those tasks where you have been unsure how to get started. The important thing is to make a start at whatever point.
- ▓ Divide large and complicated tasks into bite-sized chunks so that they appear less formidable.
- ▓ Set your own deadlines for tasks where they are not externally imposed.

---

activity – ask yourself:

- What are the tasks over which I regularly procrastinate?
- What are the reasons for this? (They may vary between tasks.)
- What strategies can I usefully adopt to overcome my own procrastination?

---

meeting deadlines

There are five main reasons why deadlines aren't met:

- The deadline is unrealistic to start with.
- The deadline is inadequately planned for.
- The person responsible for meeting the deadline is unable to get started on the task.
- The person responsible for meeting the deadline is let down by others.
- The person responsible for meeting the deadline spends more time on the assignment than necessary.

dealing with unrealistic deadlines

The best time to counteract an unrealistic deadline is when it is being set. Leaving it until later smacks of defensiveness and risks the appearance that you are simply unable to hack the job. If you think that you are being asked to work to a deadline that isn't feasible, show that you have thought through the timescale rather than simply rejecting the proposal out of hand. Adopt a positive problem-solving attitude. Set out the stages that will need to be met in order to deliver on time, and explore whether there are any ways through the difficulty – such as additional resources which would help you to meet the required timescale – or whether it is possible for the deadline to be reconsidered. Unfortunately, deadlines are seldom set in a perfect working world and, while the timescale for a project may seem reasonable when viewed in isolation, the chances are that it will cut across other assignments that also have deadlines. One tactic you can adopt with the person setting the deadline is to ask them whether it takes priority over the other deadlines you are working to, and if so, which they would wish you to set back in order to meet the timescale on the new job. This is likely to be made more difficult when you are working for more than one boss. People tend to be less respectful of deadlines set by others.

In some circumstances there may be deadlines that are unrealistic but not subject to influence. They may arise from the requirements of external bodies, regulators or clients. If affected, the only solution is to work on the other demands on your time to free the space that will allow the deadline to be met. Once again, it is essential that you do this early enough to make a difference.

Before you start work, make sure you are completely clear what is required of you, what resources you have at your disposal, and what additional support you may call upon if necessary. Failure to deal with these issues is a frequent cause of missed deadlines.

planning to meet your deadline

OK, so you have accepted the deadline. You now need to plan your implementation of it. Break the assignment or project down into a series of stages which will lead you to a successful conclusion and try to estimate the amount of time each will take. Calculate the number of working days between now and the planned completion date and ask yourself what you will need to do each week (or each day if you are dealing with a short deadline) in order to achieve it. Build in sufficient slack to take account of unexpected events and delays, and make sure that, in estimating the time needed for each stage, you have taken account of the other commitments which have a call on your time.

As you work towards completion of your project, use the finishing point for each of the stages as a milestone – a point at which you can monitor your progress, and ensure that you are on track. Use them also to give yourself the positive reinforcement necessary to maintain motivation. If you are able to get ahead of your schedule at any time, resist the temptation to slacken off. Use the time to build in some additional flexibility at the end of the project. The tidying up elements are often the ones most likely to be underestimated.

inability to get down to the work

This tendency frequently accompanies poor planning. It may be that you are not sure you have all the information you need in order to make a start or just that the finish date seems such a long way off. You convince yourself that you have ample time and will be sure to get down to it in a day or two. People will often procrastinate over the start of a project because they lack confidence in their ability to succeed at it, or they are unsure where to start. If affected by this, then cast aside worries about tackling the task at the beginning, and simply pitch in at whatever point appears to be the most straightforward. The momentum you gain from making inroads into the task will usually outweigh any inefficiencies resulting from stages tackled out of order.

avoid being let down by others

Often, completion of a project or assignment will not be entirely in your hands, and you will be reliant on input from others if you are to meet your deadline. Once again good planning is the key to ensuring that others don't present problems for you. Recognize that they will have priorities of their own, which are likely to differ from yours. Let them know in plenty of time what it is you require from them and the date by which you will need their input. It generally helps to set this date a few days before you actually need it so that any laxity on their part doesn't throw out the schedule for any subsequent work you need to do with their input. Make your requirements as clear as possible so as to avoid any misinterpretation.

don't go over the top in seeking perfection

This is another failing which signals lack of confidence. It may be a matter of research or information gathering which is out of proportion with the task in hand and results in the person undertaking the task becoming bogged down and unable to see the wood for the trees. Or it may be unwillingness to let go of the project – relentlessly honing and polishing it with the aim of producing the perfect job. You need to avoid both these tendencies and recognize the point at which further effort does not produce a commensurate return.

activity – ask yourself:

■ What difficult deadlines have I been faced with recently?
■ What were the reasons for the difficulty?
■ What do I need to do in order to address the problems in future?

time management and projects

I have referred to projects several times in this chapter, and it is worthwhile spending a few minutes considering the particular demands that projects place on your time. In the context of this chapter, we shall regard the term 'project' as including any undertaking leading to a significant outcome, where successful achievement requires completion of a number of elements over a period of time. It may be an assignment you carry out entirely by yourself, or may involve the input of others.

One of the major difficulties with project activity from a time management perspective is that it has to take place alongside other work. Harking back to the breakdown of work by importance and urgency which we used earlier in this chapter, it is usually Sector B activity – important but not urgent – and for that reason may be pushed off schedule by other, more urgent pressures which are actually less important. Care in planning and tracking your projects is therefore vital.

Whole books are written on project planning and management, and there are some complex techniques necessary for handling projects with hundreds of time-critical tasks, possibly involving the input of numerous individuals or organizations. This book, concerned as it is with personal organization, clearly cannot enter that level of complexity, but there are some basic principles that apply to all projects. Any project should embody five stages:

- ▦ initiating – clarifying general aims, setting out objectives;
- ▦ planning – breaking the project down into tasks and activities; deciding in what order they should be accomplished; determining the timescale, deciding what resources are needed;
- ▦ executing – carrying out the work, co-ordinating team members, resolving difficulties;
- ▦ monitoring – ensuring the schedule is progressing according to plan; redefining, rescheduling and re-allocating resources as necessary;
- ▦ completing – finalizing the results, reviewing the outcomes.

The organizational skills required for successfully completing projects are largely those covered in other parts of this book – setting objectives, delegation, meeting deadlines, estimating time requirements – but you should give particular attention to defining tasks and the order in which they are to be carried out. This is something that requires you to ask a number of questions:

■ What activities are needed to achieve this objective?
■ In what order should they be carried out?
■ Do any of them need to be broken down into smaller tasks?
■ What resources are required to accomplish them?

The most common problem in defining tasks is a tendency to accept the first answers that come up. Don't expect, even with straightforward projects, to pull out all the answers at once. Revisit your first attempt. You are quite likely to see new elements that were not immediately apparent.

Depending on the complexity of the project, it may be necessary to identify sub-projects, each containing its own set of tasks and sub-tasks. Some tasks will be dependent on the completion of others, or may have others dependent on them. Delays in completing such tasks can throw out the whole project schedule, so it is important to clarify start and finish dates for them, and identify what room there is for slippage.

If you are planning a project which has a lot of interrelated tasks, project planning software can greatly simplify the process. It will allow you to alter timings and relationships and to add or move tasks until you are satisfied with the project schedule. You can then make use of powerful charting and tracking facilities offered by the software (see Figure 2.4). In spite of the above, it needs to be said that monitoring progress is made much simpler if you can incorporate project tasks and milestones into your normal time tracking system. For this reason a PIM is to be favoured over free-standing specialist software for those projects that are not too complicated.

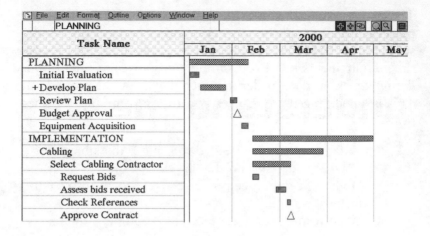

Figure 2.4 *Charting tasks and milestones with project management software*

summary

If you are to organize your time more effectively, you need to:

- ▓ be aware of the way your time is currently spent;
- ▓ be able to plan your activity over different time frames;
- ▓ select planning and tracking tools that work for you;
- ▓ estimate the time required to complete tasks;
- ▓ eliminate procrastination;
- ▓ adopt an organized approach to meeting deadlines;
- ▓ plan and track project activity.

understand the way you work

After planning and prioritizing your work and taking steps to manage your time, the next point to consider is the way in which you set about it. In this chapter, we shall examine three features of your approach to tasks which can greatly improve effectiveness: scheduling tasks at appropriate times; mobilizing the power of habit; and dealing with decisions systematically.

schedule tasks at appropriate times

It is likely that your workload consists of a variety of different tasks. You will have limited jurisdiction over when to carry out those that are dependent on the availability of others, but for the majority of tasks there will be some flexibility on timing. Most tasks will fall into one of three broad groups:

■ *maintenance tasks* – those routine jobs which are essential to keep you functioning properly, staying informed, dealing with the normal inflow and outflow

of information, organizing your workspace, filing, completing routine returns;
▪ *people tasks* – negotiating, participating in meetings, persuading, reviewing performance, networking, disciplining, presenting, training, inducting, interviewing;
▪ *creative, planning and problem-solving tasks* – preparing plans and project briefs, writing reports, analysing results and drawing conclusions, finding solutions to problems.

These are just a few examples. Depending on the nature of your job, there will be others appropriate to you.

recognize the demands that different tasks place on you

Generally speaking, the maintenance tasks will make the most limited energy demands. Later in this chapter we will look at how many of them can be made even less demanding by harnessing the power of habit. Planning and problem-solving skills will normally require the greatest amount of concentrated attention and also larger blocks of time because of the need to get yourself up to speed before you are able to make significant progress. People tasks may be of long or short duration, but are frequently the ones which make the greatest demands on emotional energy. Particularly tricky people tasks – such as disciplinary interviews or redundancy notification – may not be lengthy, but they require you to gear yourself up to deal with the possibility of unpleasant confrontation. If you have several of these tasks, try tackling them together – one after the other. The head of steam you build up to tackle the first helps to carry you through the subsequent ones and, overall, you will find it less emotionally draining than having to gear yourself up for each one individually.

We are all familiar with the idea of a body clock which regulates our sleeping and waking. Anybody who has ever worked a night shift or crossed time zones will testify to the havoc caused by its disruption. But we give much less attention to the peaks and troughs of alertness that occur throughout our waking life, and which vary significantly between individuals. Needless to say, the alertness cycles in your day can have a potent effect on performance and it pays to schedule your most demanding tasks at the times you are best able to deal with them.

what are your best times?

We are accustomed to describing ourselves in general terms – 'I'm a morning person', 'I do my best work in the evening' – but have you ever looked at your work patterns in more than the most cursory terms? You may have become locked into a way of working not particularly suited to your body rhythms as a result of difficulties in organizing your day. You may assume, for example, that evenings are the times when you do your best planning and problem-solving activity, when in fact those tasks have been squeezed into that end of the day because you have found it impossible to give them the concentrated thought they require amid the distractions and interruptions of normal working hours. If, as a result of better organization, you are able to deal more effectively with interruptions, you may find that you can readdress your assumptions about the best times to take on particular tasks.

Start by examining the way you work now. Take the following six tasks and place the relevant number for each in the chart that follows according to the approximate times when you would be most inclined to carry them out.

At what time of the day would you be most likely to:

1. arrange to meet a junior colleague who you suspect has been falsifying expenses claims;

   2. phone a customer who is threatening to take his business elsewhere because of perceived poor service from your company;

   3. plan a presentation to senior colleagues on a proposal you wish the organization to adopt;

   4. deal with your incoming mail;

   5. catch up with background reading;

   6. prepare a difficult report.

(NB If these examples are not relevant to you, select some other genuine instances from across the range of tasks you carry out.)

Time	Task
early morning	
late morning	
early afternoon	
late afternoon	
early evening	
late evening	

Now test those assumptions. Take a blank sheet of A4, long side uppermost, and divide it into three columns labelled 'Task', 'Time of day', and 'Comment'. Over a period of several days, record your responses to the significant tasks that make up your working day. Try moving some intensive tasks from the time you would normally do them to perceived periods of higher energy, and note any difference in performance.

Task	Time of day	Comment
	(am/pm/eve)	

why you can't always rely on the same body rhythms

Your normal pattern of energy peaks is a good guide to the times when you should schedule your most demanding tasks, but don't regard it as infallible. On the days when you are slightly under the weather, or at the end of an exhausting week, there may be no appreciable energy peaks and any sort of demanding activity is a struggle. If you have any choice in the matter, don't labour on with a difficult task that is not working for you. In these circumstances you are unlikely to break through into sunny pastures. Far better to switch to a more routine maintenance task and return to the intensive one when you are rested and re-energized. Beware, however, of using this as simply an excuse for procrastination.

On the reverse side of the coin, when things are going particularly well don't stop just because you have reached today's target. If you have energy and creativity to spare, and a task is flowing for you – go with it. Keep your schedules flexible and be prepared to listen to your body.

fit the task to your available time

There are some tasks that you can only set about if you have a significant chunk of time – you need to gather resources around you, get yourself into the right frame of mind and make sure that you are free of interruptions. Other tasks you can dip in and out of more quickly. Don't waste your time trying to gear up for a long-slot task when you only have a short slot available. Keep some quick pay-off tasks handy for those spare moments when somebody due for an appointment is running late, when a meeting doesn't start on time, or while you are waiting for a train.

mobilize the power of habit

You only have a finite amount of energy each day and you want to be able to expend it as productively as possible. But the chances are that all sorts of trivial and time-wasting tasks are using up your available resources and preventing you pushing forward those larger projects which require sustained concentration and effort. By enlisting the power of habit, you can free up the energy you need to devote to the intensive tasks which will really make a difference to your effectiveness. If you pride yourself in bringing an element of creativity to your work and have an instinctive antipathy towards anything that smacks of becoming a creature of habit, console yourself in the knowledge that having some habits and routines in your day can give you more energy to tackle the creative things at other times.

Consider the routines you go through when you get up in the morning – cleaning your teeth for example. They have become ingrained – part of the way you start your day. Your thoughts are elsewhere while you are doing them – listening to the radio or planning your day – and you don't worry about them. They demand no mental energy. There are tasks in your working day which can be turned into the equivalent of cleaning your teeth. They may not permit quite the same level of mental detachment, but they're tasks which currently use up unnecessary energy. They vie with all the other demands upon you for a place on your busy schedule – you have to decide when to do them, and worry about them when they are not done.

A number of the general organizational tasks featured in this book may usefully be made the subject of habits and routines. They include:

- updating your schedules for the following day/week – Chapter 2;
- handling incoming mail – Chapter 4;
- keeping desk space clear and organized – Chapter 6;
- carrying out routine filing – Chapter 7.

There will be others specific to your job. On the flip side of positive habits which can free up our energies for more important activity are current negative work habits which condemn us to ineffectiveness.

Frances Craig is a classic example of a messy desk worker. Although disciplined and organized in many other ways, she works amid overwhelming and distracting clutter. She is aware of the amount of time she wastes looking for things among the piles of paper which totally obscure her work surface, and she is conscious that with a little more discipline she could clear her desk on a daily basis and work more effectively. She engages in periodic purges during which important material is liable to get ditched with the junk, but so far she has not succeeded in building up a regular desk clearing habit.

---

what fixes habits?

Habits, positive or negative, are fixed by repetition and reinforcement. Everybody is aware of the role that repetition plays in habit formation, but often we fail to persist for long enough to make a new routine automatic. We need to remember also that repetition will only work if it is accompanied by reinforcement.

Reinforcement can be positive or negative. Often overlooked examples of positive reinforcement include a word of congratulation (even if it comes from yourself) or simply the boost that comes from crossing an item off your 'to do' list. Negative reinforcement may come in the form of unwelcome discomfort. Some reinforcers are stronger than others. Those that are clear and immediate tend to have more effect than those that are vague and in the future. In the case of Frances and her desk habits, the consequences of any different way of behaving are

vague and indefinite by comparison with the immediate reinforcement provided by her current work habit, which she
perceives as the ability to move quickly and easily from one job
to another with the minimum of preparation or clear-up time.
To change her behaviour she needs to make a deliberate
connection between different habits and their consequences,
and to work on reinforcing it every time she exhibits the
desired behaviour.

Habits are also bolstered by your environment – including
your own attitudes and perceptions of self, those close to you
and the prevailing culture in your place of work. Frances's view
of herself as a busy, creative type is a part of the background to
her behaviour, as is the tendency in her workplace to view an
empty desk as an indicator of somebody with not enough to
do.

It follows from all this that simply deciding you are going to
introduce new routines into your working day is no guarantee
of success. You need to address the environment in which your
current behaviour flourishes, and work on nurturing and reinforcing the desired habit until it becomes automatic. It won't
happen immediately but the end result will be worth a bit of
persistence.

activity – ask yourself:

▨ Which of my current work habits contribute to effective
performance of my job?
▨ What are the work habits that limit effective performance of
my job?
▨ What new habits could I develop to improve performance in
my job?

tips for changing habits

▓ Start thinking in positive terms about the habit you are working to develop. Associate it with desirable outcomes – the chance to free up time and energy for creative and enjoyable jobs – rather than focusing on the boring and mundane nature of the task itself.

▓ Similarly, associate new habits with positive aspects of your self-image – they are essential parts of your creativity and decisiveness rather than routines that bring out your bureaucratic traits.

▓ Change the environment in which those habits you wish to change currently flourish. For example, coincide a change in desk organization with an overall purge on your workspace.

▓ Remember that immediate positive reinforcement is what fixes new habits. This might come in the form of crossing an item off your 'to do' list, rewarding yourself with a desirable outcome (now I can go home, now I can go to lunch) or simply congratulating yourself on a task completed. Give yourself immediate positive reinforcement every time you engage in the new behaviour.

▓ Hang your new routines onto key times in your working day – first thing, just before lunch, immediately after lunch, just before you go home. Associating them with constant landmarks makes them less likely to be overlooked.

▓ Continue reinforcing and monitoring the new behaviour until it is established. Include the new work habit on your daily 'to do' list for several weeks and reward yourself for sticking to it.

▓ Don't try to take on too much at once – be satisfied with incremental steps, nurturing new habits until you are satisfied they are established before turning your attention elsewhere.

sharpen up your decision making

We take decisions constantly throughout the working day – what to do with each piece of paper that crosses the desk, what task to tackle next, where to seek a particular piece of information. In this chapter we are only concerned with these minor decisions insofar as they can get in the way of more major ones. If you are fussing around over trivialities or decisions that could be delegated to somebody else, then you will inevitably have less time and energy for the things that matter.

We are concerned here with those more major workplace decisions that involve serious consideration followed by commitment to a course of action which has to be seen through to a successful conclusion. You need to tackle these in an organized and systematic way if you are to be effective. There are a number of things that may get in the way of this process:

- fears and anxieties;
- availability of information and other resources;
- conflicting timescales;
- the behaviour of others.

fear

Fear, as we have already seen, gives rise to procrastination. Decisions are often postponed or referred to working groups out of fear of making a mistake. Anxiety about the process of implementing a decision may be just as important as choosing the right course of action. You may know what is the right thing to do, but the prospect of carrying it out is frightening. Possibly it holds the prospect of unpleasant encounters with others. Difficult decisions to do with people – disciplinary matters, for example – are often bucked for this reason.

information

Information is the cause of so-called 'analysis paralysis'. Either there is insufficient information to make an informed decision – often an excuse used to justify procrastination – or there is so much that the person responsible for the decision is overwhelmed. There is a fear element to information gathering too. On the one hand lies the fear that acquiring further information may throw up additional complications. On the other is the equally damaging fear that if you stop information gathering you may miss an essential nugget that would set you on the right track. You need to keep data acquisition in proportion to the importance of the issue to be decided, and learn to recognize the point at which you have obtained sufficient data to define and weigh the options adequately, without tipping over into additional work, producing rapidly declining benefits.

timing

You don't need to be told about windows of opportunity. Making the right decision at the wrong time can be as damaging as making the wrong decision at the right time. Some decisions have to be taken quickly, and dithering will allow the moment to pass. But take care not to rush decisions which need careful consideration – perhaps because there are several steps to them, or because they have implications for other activities. There may also be short- and long-term dimensions to the issue you are considering. Biting the bullet in favour of a long-term solution is generally to be favoured over repeated sticking-plaster responses.

the behaviour of others

Decisions are not taken in a vacuum. For the most part they will impact on others who will come with their full quota of prejudices, hobby horses and political baggage in the form of perceptions of status, role and reputation. They will need to be convinced of the benefits and perhaps to take ownership of the decision. Ignore all this and you might as well forget about making the decision at all.

Jill Brook is the head of a medium-sized secondary school. She is faced with a decision on the acquisition of computers for pupil use. In the past the school was advised to purchase machines that were not PC-compatible but were judged to be well served by educational software. As a result, the school has a large number of ageing machines that are unable to run software of the type pupils will find in the workplace, or increasingly in their own homes. The school has limited funds and so can only replace a proportion of the hardware in any one year. If Jill opts for a rolling programme of replacement, there will be a duality of systems and software for some years to come. By acquiring older, second-hand machines, Jill can replace a larger number of her redundant computers, but the newly acquired machines will themselves become outdated sooner, and she is concerned that they may require greater maintenance. If she chooses to buy new, she can select from budget models or more sturdy and powerful machines at greater cost. The decision she makes has other obvious ramifications such as software acquisition and training. It clearly requires a considered approach.

---

a systematic approach to decision making

There are five parts to making any serious decision:

1. clarify what you are about
This is best accomplished by asking yourself some questions:

- Why do I need to make this decision?
- What are the goals I wish to achieve?
- What information do I need to make this decision?
- What will happen if I don't do anything?
- Who do I need to involve?
- What is the timescale?
- What resources are available to me?

2. identify the available options
This is a point at which short circuits often occur. In the process of identifying options, a superficially attractive one pops up and the focus moves away from exploration of all possibilities and towards justifying why this particular solution should be chosen. Even with decisions that require a speedy response it is worth taking a little time to ensure you have identified all the possible options before you start to evaluate them.

3. weigh the pros and cons of each option
A simple approach is to adopt a balance sheet strategy for this task. Draw a line down the middle of a sheet of paper and, for each option, list the pros on one side and the cons on the other. Keep the goals of the exercise very clearly in front of you as you do this. Don't treat the pros and cons as if they all carry equal weight. You may want to give each a weighting on, say, a one to ten scale. But remember that you cannot expect to come to a conclusion simply by allocating and adding up weightings. Some points may have absolute rather than relative significance. A single point against may be of such weight that it eliminates all the points in favour. Beware also of what may seem to be overwhelming pros. The novelty value of some options may lead to the cons not being adequately explored.

4. pare the options down to the point that you are able to make a choice.

Some options will have been immediately dismissed by failing to meet the goals or having overwhelming points against them. For those that remain, you need to take account of risk surrounding their implementation. How likely is it that factors beyond your control may affect the successful implementation of the decision? And what is the balance of risk against potential gain? Also consider elements such as how the decision will be sold to those who have to implement it.

5. sell the outcome

Actually taking the decision is not the point at which the job finishes, rather the point at which it starts. It is then a matter of communicating the decision and gaining the commitment of others, and this is where a lot of good decisions come unstuck. Communicating the decision is a selling job and the principles of effective persuasion apply:

- ■ Approach the task from your audience's point of view. Address their aspirations and fears.
- ■ Establish credibility by demonstrating a clear plan for the implementation of the decision.
- ■ Sell the benefits of the decision rather than dwelling too much on the reasons for it.
- ■ Anticipate any objections that may be raised and prepare convincing responses to them.

now move on

Recognize that you can never get it right all the time, particularly when there are people involved. At the time you make the decision, its implementation lies in the future. Circumstances may change for reasons you couldn't have predicted at the time you made the decision, and for that reason you do need to keep the consequences of decisions under review. But having chosen the best option, you need to implement it and move on, without constantly revisiting the options to worry whether you have made the right choice.

analysis, emotion or intuition

When we make decisions, we are using not only our rational powers of analysis, but also our emotions, value judgements and intuition. To push these latter elements to one side may mean ignoring valuable insights. It is true that our emotions – anger, fears, likes and dislikes – may get in the way of making and implementing the right decision, but values and emotions can also help us to be sensitive to the effects of a decision on others and through that, the likelihood of its successful implementation. How many times have you intuitively known that a certain course of action was the right one or the wrong one, but been unable to put your finger on the reason why? The consequences of ignoring this little voice and proceeding solely on the basis of rational analysis can come back to haunt you.

delegate decisions

Ask yourself whether you are delegating decisions appropriately. Accepted thinking is that the responsibility for decision making should be delegated to the level closest to implementation, provided that the person concerned has the resources and authority to implement the solution. As with all delegation issues, there is frequently a reluctance to surrender authority with the result that effectiveness is lost. If you are in a position to delegate decisions, make use of the opportunity, taking account of the guidelines given in Chapter 5.

if you are genuinely stuck over a decision

You are labouring away with an intractable decision for which you simply cannot find any wholly acceptable solution. What do you do?

Come back to it. This does not have to be a cop-out and does not mean postponing the decision indefinitely. If it is possible to put off a decision for a day or two without detrimental effect, you will often find that revisiting the issues afresh allows you to see a way through the difficulty.

Find out how others may have tackled a similar problem. There may be people who can help within your own organization or professional group. For a much wider trawl of experience consider the Internet. Don't just search the World Wide Web, consider looking in Usenet too. Usenet consists of many thousands of newsgroups in which people share views on matters of common concern. Newsgroups are like electronic notice boards; you can post queries and receive responses and advice from anybody who happens to read your original message. Much of Usenet is composed of cultish and wacky groups, but there are many hundreds of professional interest groups, and the chances are that there will be newsgroups concerned with your area of work. Some professional associations now have newsgroups that are only open to designated members.

involving other people in decision making

A group approach to decision making may help to throw up more options than would be considered by an individual. It may also allow broader consideration of pros and cons. People who have been consulted are more likely to feel ownership of the preferred solution, and thus to have a greater commitment to its implementation. But the involvement of others is not an automatic plus. Groups frequently develop a culture in which assumptions are not adequately scrutinized or challenged and uncomfortable options are suppressed. This tendency, known as 'groupthink', almost inevitably leads to poor decisions, and is characterized by consensus too readily arrived at. There is also a group inclination towards decisions that are more risky than might be made by an individual, a tendency which arises from perceived greater safety in numbers. Some groups develop a gung-ho culture in which it is almost seen as wimpish to spend more than five minutes on any issue regardless of its complexity.

Another unfortunate practice is that of decisions being taken in groups because individuals wish to cover themselves in the event of anything going wrong. This is particularly common in organizations with a blame culture, where serious time and money can be wasted by groups of people sitting down to discuss issues that should rightly be left with individuals.

The same sort of 'insurance policy' tendency can be observed in the issues which individuals raise with their managers. If you suspect that the people for whom you are responsible are unnecessarily engaged in decision insurance, ask yourself whether there is anything you can do to free them up. Even in the most blame-riddled organization there is usually something you can do. Try to demonstrate that you trust your staff to make decisions, and that they will not be pilloried for mistakes when they have genuinely worked to achieve a sensible decision based on sound criteria. Sometimes it is simply a matter of people being clear about the range of their authority, or of being encouraged to let go of the protective habits acquired working for other bosses.

how much to consult

The leadership continuum originated by Tannenbaum and Schmidt is a way of looking at different levels of democracy in decision making. The range of decision making styles from autocratic to democratic can be summarized as follows:

- ▦ *Tell.* The manager makes the decision entirely alone, and simply relays it to those affected.
- ▦ *Sell.* The manager makes the decision but explains the context, reasons and benefits.
- ▦ *Test.* The manager selects a preferred course of action, but seeks out reactions before implementing it, and makes modifications if necessary.
- ▦ *Consult.* The manager sets out the problem and possible solutions before a decision is taken. The views and suggestions of those likely to be affected are solicited, but the manager retains the right to make the decision alone.
- ▦ *Join.* The manager sets out the problem and joins in the discussion on possible solutions. A consensus may emerge, but the manager has the final say on the way forward.
- ▦ *Participate.* The manager participates in a team discussion with no more authority than anybody else. A team decision emerges by consensus or majority voting.

The approach you use will depend in part on the culture of the organization you work in, your own personality and relationship with your team. But the most important determinant should be the decision to be taken. It is a mistake to slip into a preferred level of consultation which is applied irrespective of the issue under consideration. The organized manager will think about the degree of consultation appropriate to the circumstances. Telling may be the right approach for decisions where there is nothing to be gained by wider involvement or where questions of urgency or confidentiality prevent this. Joining or participating is appropriate for decisions where whole team involvement and commitment are paramount.

Remember also that consultation for the sake of appearances can be just as bad as, if not worse than, not consulting at all.

summary

Effective organization of your workload will be improved if you are able to:

- recognize those tasks which place the greatest demands on you and schedule them when you are at your most energetic;
- fit the task to the time you have available;
- build up positive work habits and eliminate negative ones;
- take a systematic approach to decisions and involve other people appropriately.

organize paperwork

- Does the amount of incoming information you are required to deal with seem to be constantly growing?
- Do you find yourself going over the same material more than once without seeming to take it in?
- Would you like to be able to read faster at the same time as improving your comprehension?
- Do you have difficulty keeping up to date with the reading you feel is necessary for effective performance of your job?
- Do colleagues bombard you with memos, reports and copies of other written material that you don't need?
- Do you find yourself unable to decide what to do with documents you receive?
- Do you put paperwork to one side to be dealt with later?
- Do you retain magazines and reports intending to read them, but never get around to it?
- Are you plagued by junk mail?
- Do you find difficulty locating a piece of information which you know is somewhere within a particular book or report?

If you haven't answered yes to any of these, then you are a pretty unusual being in today's workplace. Recent surveys have shown that throughout the developed world, people are struggling to cope with the vast quantities of information they are required to handle in their jobs and that widespread stress and productivity decline are a result.

In this chapter we will look at a systematic approach towards handling incoming paper. We will examine ways to reduce the volume of what comes your way, and techniques to help you read and assimilate it more efficiently.

identify the important information

Some information is immediately recognizable as junk. Other items scream their importance. But it isn't always simple to separate with certainty the vital from the marginal. Remember the points made in Chapter 1 about identifying the key responsibilities and objectives in your job. Use these as a form of mental checklist and match against it whatever information comes your way. You cannot be sure of getting it right every time, but resist the temptation to deal with this uncertainty by a strategy of 'if in doubt, treat it as important'. Information perfection – always having exactly the right information available at the right time – is not possible. While the availability of good information is important to the effective discharge of your job, more information will not guarantee better performance. Beyond a certain point, additional information will have a declining marginal value, and information has no value at all if there is so much of it that it cannot be properly interpreted and understood. So, recognize that you have no hope of taking in everything, focus on the important, and accept that your judgement will be imperfect. Remember also the need to discriminate between the urgent and the important. Items requiring a speedy response may assume a greater importance than they deserve. An unimportant matter which has been left

unattended for several days does not become any more important because its deadline is approaching. It simply becomes
more urgent.

adopt a systematic approach

There is a common myth, perpetuated by some time management programmes, that every piece of paper should be handled
only once. It doesn't work like that in the real world. For a
variety of reasons, you might need to come back to a document. An item may genuinely need to be mulled over or put
together with other information before you can make a sensible
decision upon it. It may be more efficient to deal with some
items in context with others on the same subject. What about
the document which makes you angry? Although a response
fired off immediately may do something for your blood pressure, you are likely to produce a more effective reply, and one
less likely to escalate confrontation if you wait a day or two
until you have cooled off. Some items may need repeated
handling in the process of drafting a complex document. If it is
possible to touch a document only once, then this is clearly
what you should aim for, but don't become too hung up on the
'one touch' approach. Ensure that no document goes back onto
the pile, and that every item receives a positive action on the
first touch. This action should be one of the following five Ds,
summarized in Figure 4.1.

discard

The quickest way to become bogged down with information is
by wasting time and energy reading material of little or no
benefit to your work. So, the first question to ask yourself is
'Do I want this at all?' It should be quickly apparent if an item
has no use for you, but we are often reluctant to consider the
bin until we have waded through a document. There is also a

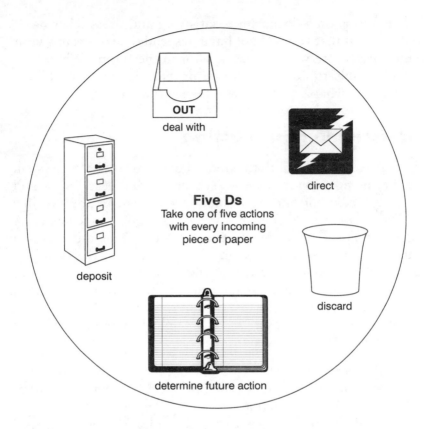

Figure 4.1   *The five Ds*

tendency to put to one side documents that one is unsure about. There they form a mounting pile with other items, gathering dust and occasionally being revisited in half-hearted attempts to clear the backlog. Remember that most information has a limited shelf life. A useful rule of thumb is – if it doesn't seem valuable today it isn't likely to tomorrow.

deal with

Provided that you are able to do so quickly and effectively, you should deal with items when they first come to you. An immediate action on a document is satisfying and stress-relieving. It also means that you will not have to spend time refreshing your memory before you can act upon it in the future. Where it is not possible to deal with an item immediately, then at least determine what action you will take and when.

determine future action

Never return an item to the pile. Make sure you have a system for bringing forward items on which you will need to act, and make a point of noting the action required, or the possible options, on the document or a sticky note attachment. A concertina file marked with the dates of the month makes a useful 'bring forward' device. Place the item in the compartment corresponding to the date when you wish to revisit it. Use project files for items which need to be worked upon with others as part of a larger task.

You will need to exert some discipline in respect of items determined for future action:

■ Do not use it to avoid one of the other four Ds.
■ Do not move items on beyond the day you have originally set for action.
■ If you have a 'to read' file, don't let it become a general dumping ground.

direct

Don't send items to others just to get them off your own desk or because you don't know what to do with them. You will only add to other people's information burden, further belabour the internal communication system and possibly fill the bins of others more quickly than your own. Think about why you are redirecting the item and what you want the other person to do with it. A brief note will help them to assimilate and act upon it more quickly.

deposit

Storing an item in whatever form of filing system is not an action to take because you don't know what else to do with it. Be sparing in what you file. We will look at ground rules for filing in Chapter 7.

Yvonne Wilkins is the finance director for a public sector organization. The prevailing culture is one in which all important communication is committed to paper and routinely copied to anybody who may conceivably have an interest. In addition to the documents central to her role, Yvonne's in tray contains an alarming number of White Papers, official reports, policy updates and guidance notes relating to the service as a whole. Yvonne considers it important to read these if she is to maintain a handle on the overall direction of the organization, and she also copies the majority of them for information to the managers who work for her. Yvonne's PA maintains a massive filing system and documents are seldom discarded. She has developed a reputation for not throwing things away and other managers and their assistants frequently turn to her when they are unable to find documents in their own systems. Yvonne regularly complains about the amount of paper that crosses her desk, but communicates with her own staff by typewritten memo, and encourages typed progress reports.

Yvonne may be working in a culture which favours over-copying and excessive use of paper communication, but there are a number of things she could do to cut down her information load. Among them are:

■ being more selective about what she reads from the material sent for her attention, particularly that which is just copied to her for information;

- ▓ discarding at first sight material of limited significance;
- ▓ limiting the amount of material she copies to others – copying just summary pages where more junior colleagues may simply need to know that a document exists;
- ▓ adopting less formal communication with her staff.

avoid overload

However effective you become at handling the stuff, you will not achieve all that is possible unless you also take steps to reduce the volume of paper which arrives daily on your desk. Even if you only glance at the majority of it, you may be wasting considerable time and effort.

The most important step you can take is to examine your own behaviour. Your maxim must be 'do unto others as you would have them do unto you'. It is particularly the case when you are communicating with junior members of staff who will take their example from you. If you aim to protect yourself by excessive copying of material to colleagues, they are likely to respond in the same way. If you routinely communicate by memo, expect to get plenty of memos back.

Here are some other ideas:

- ▓ Don't invite junk mail by handing out your business cards unnecessarily at conferences and trade fairs. And don't waste time on the junk mail you receive. You can dump the majority without even opening the envelope.
- ▓ Remove your name from mailing lists if they provide you with nothing of value.
- ▓ Consider internal communications. Circulation lists within organizations are often unnecessarily large. If you can do so without creating political difficulties for yourself, ask to be left off circulation lists for documents which do not concern you in any way.

▦ Examine subscriptions to periodicals. Those which have not yielded anything worthwhile in the last six months may be due for cancellation.

▦ If you have a secretary or assistant, get them to screen material before it is passed to you. This is in addition, not an alternative, to the other points on this list. Your secretary has no more reason to be burdened by junk mail than you have.

▦ Don't allow documents which will be routinely handled by members of your staff to be routed through you unless there is a good reason for it.

▦ UK resident individuals or organizations can eliminate junk faxes by registering free of charge with the Facsimile Preference Service (0207 766 4422). All direct marketing organizations using fax for promotion are required to be licensed by this service, and any company or individual can register their wish not to receive such material.

over-copying

Over-copying is a form of workplace insurance. When you're not sure what to do with a document or who may need sight of a memo, the easiest solution is to run off multiple copies and send them to everybody who might conceivably have use for the information therein. You have achieved two things – the offending item is off your desk, and you have also absolved yourself from any responsibility for failure to communicate. However, you have added to the information burden of others and have not necessarily communicated anything. If you aim to protect yourself by over-copying to colleagues, they are likely to respond in the same way.

If you are working in a heavily paper-based organization, you may be able to influence others to join in a campaign to reduce the amount of paper in circulation. You might, for example, raise awareness by placing a large cardboard box in a prominent position within a shared office. Over the course of a week, colleagues are encouraged to use it as a repository for all unnecessary paperwork received. As well as raising awareness, informal analysis of the contents can lead to agreement on ways to reduce needless documentation. An alternative approach is to publish photocopier totals within a department on a monthly basis and to set targets for their reduction.

To reduce the amount of reading that falls on your desk, consider a co-operative approach to major documents which may need to be assimilated by several people within the organization. Colleagues agree to take it in turns to be the lead reader of weighty reports or new guidelines. Each does the donkey work on a particular document and provides the others with a summary.

read more efficiently

The speed and efficiency with which you can assimilate incoming information is a significant factor in your ability to organize your workload. It has been estimated that people in information-intensive jobs may spend up to a third of their working day in activities involving reading, and yet most of us are not as efficient readers as we might be. The average reading speed is between 200 and 250 words a minute. With some simple techniques and practice this can easily be raised to 500+ without detriment to your understanding. Slow reading speeds are not particularly a function of education or intelligence. Many able and well-educated people read at or below the average speed. Even if you already read quickly, there is generally scope for improvement. It is a myth that only by reading slowly can we expect to understand material. Better comprehension can go hand in hand with faster reading.

what is my current reading speed?

If you want to estimate your reading speed, simply choose an appropriate passage, at least a page in length, that you haven't previously read. Try to read it at a normal pace consistent with understanding the content, but take an accurate note of the time it takes you. Next, estimate the length of the passage by multiplying the average number of words per line by the number of lines it contains. Use the following calculation to estimate your reading speed in words per minute.

$$\frac{\text{number of words in the passage} \times 60}{\text{time taken in seconds}} = \text{reading speed in words per minute}$$

why do we read slowly?

When we read, our eyes do not move continuously across the page, but rather hop several words at a time through the material. It is during the stationary period (fixation) at the end of each hop that the reading occurs; and it is, of course, the brain which does the reading rather than the eyes. In simple terms, we might think of the eyes as a still camera taking a series of shots which the brain then interprets. The main reasons for slow reading speed are:

■ limited number of words encompassed in each fixation;
■ fixations of longer duration than necessary;
■ involuntary or deliberate back skipping over material already read.

A fourth factor in slow reading is a tendency to mentally hear the words as we read. This is known as sub-vocalization and is believed to originate from the approach used when we first learn to read – actually speaking the words aloud. The problem with sub-vocalization is that it restricts us to little more than the speed of the spoken voice which is typically around 150 words a minute. Sub-vocalization can be greatly diminished if never entirely eliminated.

Training yourself to read faster is a matter of technique and practice. There are numerous books and courses available on the subject, and in the space available here, it is only possible to introduce a few techniques. With a little determination these should bring about a significant improvement.

using a pacer

Most speed reading programmes advocate training with some form of pacing technique which forces your eyes to move on and eliminates lengthy pauses or back skipping. You can use your index finger or the blunt end of a pencil, moving it swiftly across the page just below the line of text you are reading (Figure 4.2). At the end of the line, move the pacer quickly to the start of the next line, and so on. Maintain a pace above that which feels comfortable and refuse to allow your eyes to go back over what you have already read. At first you may feel that you have taken in little or nothing of what your eyes have passed over, but with practice you will find increased levels of comprehension as well as speed. It has been shown that faster readers actually understand more because they are able to tune in to the general thrust of the piece they are reading, whereas slower readers become bogged down in detail.

It is natural to feel some anxiety about the process of taking in larger blocks of material at each hit, but in many aspects of our daily lives we absorb significant blocks of information at a glance. We register road signs, hoardings and headlines without stopping to 'read' them and we can significantly increase the span of words which we take in on each fixation. It is commonly thought that fast readers read down the middle of the page and that their span therefore encompasses the whole

Figure 4.2 *A pacer*

line of text. This is, however, very difficult to achieve except with text in columns. Fast readers may take in six or more words per fixation, and their eyes will remain in the central third of the page rather than following a line down the centre of it.

As your reading speed increases, you should find yourself able to progress to a smooth zigzag movement of the pacer, taking in more than one line at each pass, and without the necessity to lift the pacer from the page (Figure 4.3). Avoid reaching the point where you are forcing yourself along and are more conscious of the process of reading quickly than of what you are taking in. Once you have reached a reasonable speed you may wish to relinquish your pacer.

Figure 4.3 *As speed increases, adopt a smooth zigzag motion with the pacer*

other techniques

Increasing your reading speed will, of course, take a little time and you may wish to tap into the structured practice of a speed reading course. Whether or not you choose to do so, here are some further techniques you can employ almost immediately to improve both speed and understanding.

preview for increased understanding

We read much more quickly and effectively if we are slotting information into a known framework. A few moments spent establishing that framework can pay significant dividends. The approach which follows assumes you are setting out to read a substantial document such as a book, periodical or report. It can be adapted for shorter documents:

1. Before starting on the main text, skim through the Contents page, Introduction and Summary (if there is one) or Conclusions.
2. Next, flick through the document, establishing an appreciation of the main structure and argument. Look particularly for section or chapter summaries. They are excellent for getting quickly to the guts of a document. Failing that, read the first and last paragraph of each section or chapter. These will often introduce and summarize the arguments contained therein.
3. Now, when you move to read the document properly, you will be filling in the gaps rather than starting with a blank sheet. You will know which are the parts you need to concentrate on, and which you can blast through or skip altogether.

vary your pace

It goes without saying that texts vary in their levels of difficulty, but many people maintain the same pace regardless of what they are reading. Even within a document there will be some sections which are more difficult to absorb than others. Don't be afraid to slow down where the text requires it, and to power through the easier passages.

focus on what is important

At some point in most documents there will be digressions from the main argument, things which you already know, things you don't need to know and straightforward padding. The best way to approach any reading task is with the question 'What do I need from this?' foremost in your mind. You will read more quickly and remember more, if you can focus on the elements which are necessary for you in whatever task you have to fulfil. Don't approach the printed word with too much reverence. The writer does not necessarily know any more than you do on the subject.

get the environment right

Your reading efficiency is affected by your surroundings and feelings. Ensure that lighting is adequate and distractions are minimized. Long stretches of reading from computer screens are particularly wearing, so take care to adjust the contrast and brightness for maximum comfort and take more frequent breaks than you would with paperwork. Opt for a larger monitor for more comfortable viewing and go to a full screen view to get more of the text on screen at once. In Microsoft Word, for example, you will get approximately a third more text on the screen by choosing 'Full Screen' from the 'View' menu – useful when you are proofing long documents.

develop scanning techniques

When you need to find a particular piece of information, you can move to it quickly by scanning. Focus your attention solely on the information you wish to locate and let your eyes follow your finger as you run it rapidly down the centre of each page from top to bottom. This process should be considerably faster than your paced reading, and if you are focused on the information you want to locate, it should leap out at you when you get to the relevant part of the document. You will improve with practice. Of course, scanning is no substitute for using an index where one exists.

be selective about what you read

Never try to read everything that lands on your desk. That way lies madness. You need to be ruthlessly selective and stick to those things which add value to your role. And remember – the person who puts reading matter aside for an indeterminate time in the future when they will be less busy is destined to be forever disappointed.

use your memory

The value of what you read declines pretty rapidly if you can't remember it. Fear of forgetting results in a number of negative habits. We hang on to documents of minor significance, read slowly and back skip over the printed page. For effective information handling we need to trust our memories. The more we use them, the more reliable they will be. If you do nothing to assist your memory you will forget up to 80 per cent of what you read within 24 hours of reading it. Here are a number of simple techniques which can help you remember better:

■ The level of recall you require will vary. For some information, it will be sufficient for you to remember simply that it exists and where to find it. With other information you will need a grasp of the general subject and main ideas. At the highest level you may need to recall information in detail or even verbatim. Assist your memory by selective reading and awareness of the level of recall you need.

■ Read with a question in your mind. What do I want to achieve from this? How does it fit into what I know already? All learning and remembering is a process of association.

■ Try to see the overall pattern to what you are reading. We remember much better if we can see the general structure and the broad ideas into which the detail fits.

■ Use the information in some way. Summarize it in your own words, make margin notes as you read, communicate the information to others, or act on it.

▥ Recognition, the process of remembering with assistance from an external stimulus, is much easier than pure recall. Make conscious associations which will help you to pull detail from your memory. It has been shown that the more bizarre the association, the more likely it is to work. Silly mnemonics, ridiculous visual associations, they all work.

▥ Review important information to fix it in your long-term memory. You will gain the most advantage by quickly reviewing material shortly after acquiring it (10 to 15 minutes) and again a day later. Experts recommend further review after a week and a month for reliable long-term recall.

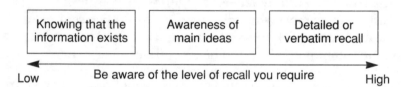

Figure 4.4 *Level of recall*

summary

Dealing effectively with paper is a matter of:

▥ separating the important information from the junk;
▥ maintaining a systematic approach with all incoming paper;
▥ handling all incoming paperwork as sparingly as possible;
▥ taking steps to reduce unnecessary incoming mail;
▥ building up your reading speed and comprehension;
▥ using memory techniques and review to assist your recall.

organize the way you work with others

Much of our working day is spent in some form of interaction with others. The way you approach these interactions can have a considerable impact on your effectiveness. In this chapter we shall look at meetings, delegation, overcoming distractions and interruptions, helping others to be more organized, and learning to say no.

a strategy for meetings

The time-wasting potential of meetings is immense. In many organizations you can spend hours every week in meetings that achieve very little. But for all that we moan about them, we keep on holding the things and attending them. Why?

People go to meetings for reasons other than to make decisions. Meetings cultivate a sense of one's importance – closeness to the wheels of power. They are an opportunity to make an impression on your colleagues. Not being invited may smack of exclusion. I have known people, left out of meetings that had almost negligible relevance to them, become incandescent over what they perceived as deliberate downgrading attempts. There is also a social element to meetings, and they can be less demanding than some other forms of work activity. Once you are in the meeting you're cocooned, safe from phone calls, interruptions and the tough problems that inhabit your in tray. OK, so meetings are boring, but you can play a few mind games with colleagues or just let your attention wander.

Why do we hold meetings? Meetings are held to:

■ impart information;
■ elicit views;
■ stimulate new ideas;
■ motivate a team;
■ reach decisions.

There are more effective ways of passing on information than dragging people together into a room and subjecting them to one of those verbal memo meetings where only the senior person speaks and everybody else sits mute. There are also non-meeting ways of consulting and eliciting views. We will look at some of them later. The creative or brainstorming meeting has long been seen as a way of exploring new solutions to problems, but studies have shown that frequently people are more creative when working individually. Similarly, one-to-one reinforcement and coaching can often achieve more than a motivational team meeting, and we have seen in Chapter 3 that meetings may have drawbacks when it comes to making decisions.

So, in the face of all this, whenever the prospect of a meeting comes up, the first question to ask yourself is: *Do we need a meeting at all?* Unfortunately that question isn't asked often enough. In many organizations, meetings go ahead at regular intervals regardless of whether they are really needed. Business expands to fill the agenda and you have all the ingredients of a classic talking shop.

Given that the answer to the 'do we need a meeting' question is yes, what can you do to ensure that a meeting achieves its purpose without devouring too much of the participants' time? Unproductive meetings generally fall down on aspects of planning and management.

inadequate planning

There may be no agenda, a poorly prepared one, or no clear purpose to the meeting. Information needed to make sensible decisions may not have been produced, or participants may have failed to read papers provided in advance.

poor management

There may be inadequate control of timing, failure to keep discussion on the agenda, inability to control people intent on riding their pet hobby horses, inability to draw conclusions out of the discussion.

Here are some pointers aimed at overcoming these and other meeting problems.

ten points to remember when calling a meeting

1. Frame the agenda as clearly as possible. Identify the specific questions the meeting needs to address rather than setting open-ended topics.
2. Indicate a target time allowance for each agenda item and stick to it as closely as you can.
3. Limit attendance to those who have something to contribute on the matters under discussion and the authority to implement decisions. Generally speaking, the more people there are at a meeting, the longer it will take.

4. Schedule meetings immediately before lunch or at the end of the day. People's anxiety to get away will override their verbosity.

5. Try not to schedule meetings in your own office. They may be subject to 'important' interruptions, and you will find it harder to get away from any post-meeting hangers-on.

6. Start the meeting at the scheduled time. Waiting for latecomers encourages them to repeat the misdemeanour, and irritates those who have arrived on time.

7. Don't allow discussion to be sidetracked onto matters not on the agenda. If they are important they can be dealt with at a subsequent meeting.

8. Don't waste time discussing matters where there is inadequate information to make a decision. Agree responsibility for obtaining and reporting the necessary information and postpone the discussion to a future date.

9. Avoid the practice of Any Other Business at the end of meetings if at all possible. It is often used by people too lazy to prepare an item properly for the agenda, and can result in bad decisions made on the basis of inadequate consideration. It can also kick into touch all your efforts at timing discussion.

10. Ensure that as soon as possible after the meeting, a record of the outcomes is prepared. The quicker it is done, the easier the task. Detailed minutes are generally unnecessary, and only give people something to argue over at the start of the next meeting. Action notes are more useful. They should include: a) what the meeting agreed; b) who has responsibility for actioning those agreements; and c) dates by which they should be actioned.

ten points to remember when attending a meeting

1. Make sure beforehand that you know what the meeting is aiming to achieve. If the aim doesn't seem clear, question the convenor about it. This should have the effect of clarifying objectives, leading to a more productive meeting, or demonstrating that a meeting isn't actually needed.

2. Ask to be excused any meeting which does not appear to have any relevance to you. You have to be wise to the politics of this. If your boss is the one calling the meeting, diplomacy may require that you go. Often, however, the convenor simply hasn't given sufficient thought to meeting membership. Questions like, 'What are you hoping I will be able to contribute?' can cause them to think again.

3. If only one item in a meeting is relevant to you, ask whether it can be placed near the beginning of the agenda so that you can be spared the rest of the meeting. Be aware though, that this tactic sometimes sparks a bidding war on the part of others similarly affected.

4. Always read the agenda and papers before a meeting and, without taking up an inflexible position, clarify your thoughts as to what you would like to achieve from the meeting.

5. If you expect your arguments to meet with some opposition, a little subtle lobbying in advance may be useful. Other participants may not have given the meeting much advance thought, and people are more inclined to stick with a view that they take into the room than they are to be won over by something they hear during the meeting. Handle lobbying carefully though. If the other person sees your approach as an attempt to exert undue influence, you risk

actually turning them away from your point of view.

6. Think in advance about what you will settle for if you don't get what you want. Most people will not have thought about a fallback position. Skilfully presented – that is before it is apparent to everyone that you have lost the argument – it can be a disarming way of getting at least a substantial part of what you want.

7. Don't overcommit yourself. Meetings are a bit like auctions. In the to and fro of discussion it's easy to get carried away and make undertakings you later regret. There's a natural wish to make a good impression in front of colleagues, but don't let yourself be tempted into taking on too many responsibilities or offering unrealistic target dates for completion of work.

8. If you find yourself locked into excessively long meetings, arrange for an 'important' appointment, or vital interruption, which will require you to leave before the end. Don't do it too often, or you will arouse suspicions.

9. You can help a weak chairperson by summarizing the arguments of others and pulling the threads of a discussion together to facilitate decisions. By all means draw people's attention to overruns on time, but take care to ensure that you are not a guilty party. We tend to overestimate the time that other people have been talking and underestimate our own loquacity.

10. Try to set some regular times when you are available for meetings attendance and make them known. If you are able to make this work, it can help prevent meetings breaking up your working week in such a way that you are unable to get to those tasks which require concentrated activity over a number of hours.

alternatives to meetings

As noted at the beginning of this section, there are more efficient ways of doing some of the business traditionally reserved for meetings, and these can be assisted by modern technology. E-mail communication can replace some meetings which are solely about information dissemination and consultation. The latest versions of Outlook e-mail software even allow senders to include voting buttons in a message to facilitate the collection of views. Internet conferencing takes the possibilities further. Microsoft Net Meeting allows you to hold a full-scale meeting with the opportunity for participants to exchange views in real time by typing them on a chat board, or via an audio link (although this permits conversation between just two people at a time). Ideas can be illustrated on a whiteboard, and applications on one computer shared with the others.

Video conferencing offers a further level of sophistication. The hardware required for this is now cheap and readily available – consisting of a camera, video capture card and conferencing software (for each participant). However, at normal modem speeds, picture quality and the rate at which it is possible to display video frames is very poor. A fast Internet connection is really a necessity.

delegate

Edward Norton reckons to work an average 60-hour week. He has a wide-ranging role in an organization which has been going through major changes over the last two years. Edward's job has been closely associated with those changes and he is concerned that he spends far too much of his time firefighting. He is aware that he doesn't delegate enough to the seven people who report to him. Some of them are more effective than others, and he feels that those he can trust are already overloaded. At present there are some tasks he does very efficiently that he knows he should delegate but, viewed on a month-by-month basis, the time taken to brief and coach somebody else would exceed the time he is currently spending on the tasks. In a situation of change, he is also unsure how long his workload will remain at the present level, and hence is reluctant to pass on responsibilities only to take them back later. At the back of his mind there is even a slight worry that he may need his heavy workload to justify his existence in any future restructuring. From time to time he gets so overloaded that he simply has to dump jobs on his colleagues with wholly insufficient briefing or assistance.

There are lots of Edwards in every area of work – people whose competence is being stretched to the limit by competition, change and restructuring. They are suffering from the catch-22 situation where they know they ought to delegate more but haven't the time to do it properly. But for anybody who wants to get organized and stay on top of their job, delegation has to be part of the recipe. It is an essential and important part of what a manager should be doing.

The first important point about delegation is that it should not be a knee-jerk reaction to your own overload. It isn't a matter of offloading tasks you don't want to do, but a contribution to overall productivity by placing responsibility and the necessary authority and resources where they can be discharged most effectively. You will have difficulty in delegating if you can't trust the people who work for you, or if you cannot believe that anyone else is able to do the job as well as you.

four steps to effective delegation

1. decide what you will delegate

The choice of responsibilities to delegate will normally centre on those things which others may do more quickly, more cheaply or more expertly than you, or tasks which can readily be performed within the context of another person's existing job. There are clearly core elements to any manager's job which should not be delegated. They are likely to include such things as: strategic planning, team leadership, appointment and appraisal of immediate subordinates. There may also be legal or company requirements for particular responsibilities to be handled personally by a named manager.

2. choose the right person
Beware of the natural tendency to load the willing horses, or to delegate tasks only to those who have fulfilled similar work in the past. Think about people who have perhaps not had the opportunity to show what they can do. The reasons for delegation are not only about easing your own workload but about giving new development experiences to others.

3. prepare the ground
You have to be ready to spend some time preparing colleagues for what you want them to do. Time to achieve this is often an issue for busy managers, but it is a matter of short-term pain for long-term gain. If you don't set the arrangement up properly, you are likely to have disgruntled colleagues feeling they have been dumped on, or people unclear about what is expected of them. You will need to:

3a. set the objectives
The person to whom you are delegating responsibility needs to know what is expected of them and what the reporting arrangements are. Set clear objectives using the SMART formula which we discussed in Chapter 1. Let your colleagues know the parameters of their authority and what support you will be able to provide. Remember that there may be elements of coaching required before a colleague is equipped to take on a new responsibility.

3b. sell the benefits

Look at these from the other person's point of view. There may be training and development benefits in taking on a new responsibility, enhancement of career prospects, variety and challenge, or opportunity to use particular skills. Be prepared to spend time talking to the person concerned, seek responses to what you are proposing, and respond to them constructively. If your colleagues can feel that the setting up process is a collaborative one, they will be more committed to taking it on.

3c. give the necessary authority and resources

This is often the most difficult aspect of delegation. You want somebody to take on a responsibility, but you are reluctant to let go of the reins. You must do so. If you don't it will remain essentially your responsibility, for which you have simply contracted out part of the donkey work. When problems occur, they will wind up back on your plate, and your colleague will not achieve the development benefits that delegation can offer. People almost invariably perform better if they know they are trusted. Cast aside any sense of insecurity and recognize that you have to give others the opportunity to do the job. It's what management is all about.

4. stand back, report back, feedback

Let them get on with it. One of the biggest delegation problems – again a difficulty in letting go – is a tendency for the senior person to interfere or reject the work because it is not being done in exactly the way they would have done it. You need to work hard to avoid this, particularly if you have been doing the job yourself for some time. You should make it clear that you are available to offer support but that day-to-day responsibility is down to the person to whom you have delegated it. Of course, the authority you delegate is not limitless, and the person taking on the responsibility should be aware of its limits, but he or she also needs the freedom to operate and sometimes to make mistakes and learn from them.

The objectives you set should have included arrangements for your colleague to report back, and these should be opportunities for you to question and make sure that the task is on track. In these sessions, or at any other time the opportunity arises, give immediate positive feedback on those aspects of performance that are leading to the desired results. I cannot overemphasize the importance of this. People's behaviour is shaped much more strongly by positive feedback on the things they are doing well than by being chewed off about the things they are doing badly. That does not mean that you should ignore things that might not be working out as planned, but you need to concentrate on helping your colleagues to rectify any shortfall in performance. Your overriding objective is to have them fulfilling delegated responsibility consistently well so that you can concentrate on the other parts of your own job.

tracking delegated responsibilities

A common fault among disorganized managers is the tendency to forget what they have delegated to whom, and to lose track of objectives set and timescales allocated. Few things engender greater disillusion in the mind of the person to whom the work has been delegated. You need to ensure you remain on top of responsibilities allocated. Make notes of your discussions and keep them in a file for that member of staff, so that you can remind yourself of the objectives before any feedback session. Tasks and target dates along with the names of people to whom they have been assigned can be entered in the 'to do' section of a personal information manager (PIM). For more complex allocation and tracking of tasks within projects, you may want to consider the use of project management software.

reverse delegation

This is a euphemistic way of referring to the process whereby a more junior colleague comes to see you with a problem which you have delegated to them, or is firmly within the scope of their job, and you end up taking it on. It is clearly something to be avoided at all costs.

When somebody comes to you with a problem and you are too busy or distracted to give it your attention there and then, the easiest thing to say is, 'Leave it with me'. It's a convenient tactic for getting rid of them, but their problem is now your problem. Even if you subsequently succeed in handing it back to them, you have acquired the responsibility for taking the next action on the problem, and you will probably have to spend some valuable time refocusing on it before you can carry out that action.

There are some people who, without any encouragement on your part, are particularly adept at transferring responsibility upwards, and you will need to work hard to train them out of the habit. You can immediately recognize what they are up to by the language they use: 'We've got a problem here', or 'I thought you would want to handle this one'. There is a natural tendency to be flattered by their confidence in your expertise, and perhaps to feel guilty at leaving a junior colleague with a stressful problem. But resist the temptation to take it on unless the problem is clearly within your domain. Your role is to provide support and advice, but at the end of the discussion, your colleagues should be in no doubt that the problem is still their responsibility. Remember that you do them no favours by taking the problem on yourself. Only by working it through themselves, with appropriate support from you, can they develop the skills and confidence to tackle future difficulties.

sideways delegation

In these days of flatter management structures, a new term – sideways delegation – has begun to appear. This is really more about trading responsibilities than delegating them in the accepted sense. We all have differing skills and work preferences. If a colleague is able to fulfil an area of your responsibility more effectively than you, and you in turn can bring your skills to an aspect of his or her job, then it makes sense to co-operate. However, the fact that the arrangement is between colleagues at the same level should not be a reason for any less care in setting it up. The principles of clear objectives and regular feedback apply just as much as in other forms of delegation.

overcoming distractions and interruptions

Brian Adamson is a solicitor specializing in conveyancing work. It is most important that he is able to spend protracted periods of time and give his full attention to working through the documents associated with the transactions he is handling. For his clients, the sale or purchase of their property is often a source of considerable stress, and he is plagued by people arriving without appointments or phoning to speak to him urgently. He knows from experience that refusing to take the call can lead to further problems, but he finds that even short interruptions may seriously disrupt his concentration.

Interruptions and distractions impose heavily on ability to organize work schedules. Not only is there the actual time lost through the interruption but, more importantly, the effort of getting back to the original task and refocusing attention. Some interruptions will occur for genuine business reasons while others are more social, often by people who are themselves engaged in procrastination over tasks they want to escape. You may even be the source of the interruption. It is very easy to convince yourself that you just have to make a phone call or get a coffee, and that you will be back on the task in a few minutes.

Once the pattern of work is disrupted, you find other pressing chores and the minutes stretch to an hour or more, after which time it is much harder to pick up the threads.

You will never be able to get rid of interruptions entirely, but you can do a lot to reduce them, and to make those remaining as brief and purposeful as possible. Aim to cut out all bar the most urgent and important – those things which impinge on the key purpose of your job or the organization you work for, and where the consequences of failure to give the matter your immediate attention may be of detriment to either.

ten ways to reduce interruptions

1. If you are fortunate enough to have an assistant or secretary, part of the job should be to field your callers and phone calls. Scheduling a session with your assistant at the start of each day, when you go through appointments and priorities for the day, is a useful way of limiting interruptions on the assistant's part. Discuss with your assistant which situations are sufficiently important for you to be interrupted, and help with some convincing lines for dealing with the rest.

2. If you don't have the benefit of an assistant, explore a reciprocal arrangement with colleagues whereby you divert your phone to others so that they can take messages for you when you need to work on a task uninterrupted. You, of course, do the same for them at other times.

3. Failing either of these possibilities, disable the ringing tone on your phone when you want to be undisturbed and use voicemail or an answering machine to collect your messages. It helps in these circumstances to have another number, perhaps the number of a close colleague, which people can ring in the event of an urgent message.

4. Set regular times each day when you will deal with those tasks which require uninterrupted concentration and will be unavailable for meetings, calls and other interruptions. Stick to it rigidly and others will come to recognize it.

5. Be firm with self-generated interruptions. Recognize them as time-wasting habits.

6. Help to foster a climate conducive to effective work by treating colleagues as you would have them treat you. Don't expect people to refrain from interrupting you, if you are in the habit of interrupting them.

7. Take breaks at predetermined times. Build them into one of the constructive work routines which we looked at in Chapter 3, so that they start to work against self-inflicted interruptions.

8. Consider taking half a day or a day to work from home when you have a task which needs concentrated thought. Provided that your home doesn't have its own distractions, you can achieve more in a few hours of peace than you thought possible. Any boss with half a brain should realize that results matter more than where the work is carried out. Unfortunately there are still some dinosaurs around who regard working from home as a skive.

9. Group small tasks such as telephone calls together, to avoid them becoming separate interruptions to your flow.

10. If you have the sort of boss who considers that his or her every summons constitutes a reason for you to drop everything, be prepared to work patiently and diplomatically to improve awareness of the effects of such behaviour. Share with the boss, at times other than when interrupting you, the measures you are taking to manage your day and demonstrate the effectiveness of your strategy by your results.

open door or closed door

Anybody who tries to operate an open door policy at all times deserves every interruption they get, but by going to the other extreme you may seriously limit accessibility and the opportunity to remain in touch with what is happening in your area of responsibility.

Think about setting times each day when your door is open. Half an hour morning and afternoon should be sufficient. At other times people wanting to see you need to make a specific appointment. Make your 'surgery' times well known and stick to them. Even if you work in an open-plan environment and have no door to shut, you can still operate this arrangement, perhaps using an 'OK to disturb/Please do not disturb' card by your desk.

keeping interruptions brief and productive

When interruptions are unavoidable, aim to make them as short as possible. Here are some ideas:

▨ Put a time limit on the interruption. Let the person interrupting you know that you can only spare, say, five minutes. Some experts suggest keeping an egg timer on your desk and using it to remind your visitor to get to the point quickly.

▨ Risk being considered rude by not inviting interrupters to sit down.

▨ Position office furniture and desk to avoid giving your working area a 'please walk in and sit down' appearance. This is particularly important if you are in an open-plan office.

▨ Encourage colleagues to come with a bullet point note of what they want to talk to you about. This helps you to tune into the issue quickly, helps them to focus their thinking, and deters more frivolous interruptions because of the preparation involved.

■ If you have difficulty drawing interruptions to a conclusion and sending visitors on their way, think about your body language, and the verbal cues within a conversation that allow you to wrap the meeting up without unduly offending the other person.

help others to be more organized

In spite of all your attempts to organize your own schedule and way of working, the disorganization of others can still throw you into confusion, so it's worth giving some attention to strategies for greater organization among those around you.

if they work for you

Lecturing people on their lack of organization will seldom lead to much more than grudging compliance and, as none of us are wholly without fault, it will often be accompanied by privately exchanged grumbles of, 'He/she's a fine one to talk'. Getting people to articulate their own difficulties and the tactics they can adopt to resolve them is likely to be far more productive. This is generally a matter of asking the right questions in a setting which encourages reflection – a one-to-one meeting or appraisal, for example. Help your colleagues to focus on one thing at a time, and give immediate positive reinforcement in the form of praise and encouragement when you see them working to change their ways. Reinforcement is a very powerful motivator for change, so don't wait until the altered behaviour hits you between the eyes. Actively look for things to praise. Peer pressure can also be a strong influence on individual behaviour. It may be worth considering whether there is mileage in a whole team initiative aimed at working towards improved effectiveness.

if you work for them

A disorganized boss can be a nightmare to work for, but don't treat his or her weaknesses simply as gripes to be shared with other colleagues over coffee. Provided you go about it the right way, you can make a difference, but you will need to be content to work on those aspects of your boss's behaviour that you can influence, and put up with those you can't. Make sure that your own work and organization cannot be faulted, and avoid full-frontal challenges unless you have another job to go to. Here are five traits frequently displayed by disorganized bosses with suggestions on what to do about them.

inability to make a decision

Remember that bosses are seldom masters of their own destiny. Rather than fuming over what might seem at first sight to be indecisiveness and negativity, make an attempt to understand the politics in which they are operating, and give them the ammunition to fight battles further up the line. Recognize also that your boss may have difficulty tuning in to an issue which has been the focus of your attention for days or even weeks. Be prepared to talk through the thought processes which have led to the conclusions you have reached.

a tendency towards snap decisions

This species lies at the other end of the scale from the indecisive boss and will deal with any question by delivering top-of-the-head certainties. Anything that smacks of thinking time or consideration of alternatives is for wimps. Never approach such a boss with an open-ended question unless you want to find yourself saddled with unworkable solutions and impossible deadlines. Work out the options beforehand and present them with a cogently argued thumbnail guide. The boss will normally want to be credited with a decision, so build in at least one point where there is a choice to be made between alternatives, neither of which would be disastrous.

inability to end meetings

If your boss is the sort of person who finds it difficult to conclude a meeting, make sure that you have another pressing engagement which allows you an escape route within a reasonable time.

failure to set clear objectives or focus on the important issues

Clarify your aims and objectives by writing down what you think they are and getting your boss to confirm them. In one-to-one meetings with your boss, provide a written summary of the issues for discussion and a range of the possible solutions.

inability to remember what he or she has asked you to do

Develop a practice of taking notes whenever you meet to discuss tasks, and sending your boss an action note detailing what you have agreed to do, as soon as possible afterwards.

learn to say 'no'

A large part of organizing yourself is about remaining in control of your workload. If you always say 'yes' to requests that come your way, then you lose that control. You overburden yourself, with the resultant stress, and by saying 'yes' to unimportant requests you may find yourself unable to fulfil key features of your job. There are a number of reasons why saying 'no' may be difficult:

▓ You don't want to appear unwilling and spoil your career prospects.

▓ You're concerned that you might displease others or hurt their feelings.

▓ You underestimate the increased pressure you will be under as a result of saying 'yes'.

▓ You simply don't realize that saying 'no' is an option.

Of course, you don't want to get a reputation as somebody who is negative and work-shy – a knee-jerk 'no' is worse than a knee-jerk 'yes'. If you are in the process of establishing yourself in the job, you may need to say 'yes' more often than is good for you. But it is important to be able to draw the line skilfully and assertively, and recognize that it is impossible to please everyone all the time. Decide which requests you need to turn down by asking yourself:

▓ Does this comprise a core element of my job?

▓ Will my career prospects be affected if I don't do it?

▓ What else might I need to drop or postpone in order to undertake this? What will be the effect of that on other elements of my job?

▓ Will doing it result in any detrimental lifestyle effect – significantly increased stress, unreasonable intrusion on my leisure time?

▓ Will I miss out on any opportunity to develop a new skill if I don't do this?

Try a balance sheet approach – pluses on one side, minuses on the other – where the choice is difficult.

how to do it

There are three ways of approaching 'no'.

aggressive approach
Complains loudly about being overburdened and taken for granted. Accuses the person making the request of being unreasonable, rants or bursts into tears.

timid approach
Responds to the request with mumbled attempts to delay a decision. Leaves the person making the request unclear about whether 'yes' or 'no' has been said. Wastes energy fretting about the request and ends up doing it resentfully.

assertive approach
Indicates pleasure at being asked, but explains succinctly and politely why he or she is unable to respond positively. Suggests possible alternative ways of getting the task done, and specifies what support he or she can offer to whoever takes on the task.

Needless to say, the third is the approach you should aim for. The person making the request is under no misapprehension about your response or the reasons for it, but does not come away from the encounter angry and brow-beaten; and you do not damage your reputation for helpfulness and positive thinking.

Take particular care with requests where the commitment asked of you is not immediate, but comes at some time in the future – a request to deliver a paper at a conference, for example. When the event is three months away, it's easy to be over-optimistic about the time you will have to fit in the necessary preparation. But as the day approaches and you find your schedule ever more crowded, the additional task assumes the status of unwelcome addition to a heavy workload, and you end up resentfully turning out a rush job which doesn't do you justice. Awareness of priorities, clarity about your schedule and control over planning are the ways to ensure that you don't fall into this trap.

summary

You can achieve greater effectiveness in those aspects of your work that involve others by:

- helping to ensure that the meetings you attend are as productive as possible, whether you are in the chair or simply a participant;
- delegating in the right way and for the right reasons;
- actively working to beat distractions and interruptions;
- recognizing that you can help others to be more organized;
- learning to say no assertively.

organize your office space

The way you organize your office space can have a considerable effect on your productivity – saving time, preventing fatigue, allowing you to complete tasks more quickly. But it's very easy to become accustomed to a working environment that is less than ideal, so take a few minutes to look at your office with a fresh eye:

- How often do you have to get up from your chair to retrieve things that are out of reach?
- Is there space and absence of clutter on your desktop to allow you to work comfortably and without distraction?
- Are your computer keyboard and monitor positioned so that you can use them comfortably and without undue fatigue?
- Is there space adjacent to your computer workstation for any papers you need while you are working at it?
- Are your cupboards, drawers and bookcases crammed with items you don't need?
- Is your storage equipment appropriate for the items you need to keep in it?

- Do you regularly have to spend time searching for things?
- Is your office furniture best positioned for your different needs – working at your desk, using the computer, meeting with colleagues or customers?

There is no standard recipe for organizing your office space – what feels comfortable to you may not to somebody else – but there are some general principles that you should consider in arriving at the best arrangement for you.

think about ergonomics

Ergonomics is the process of designing machines, work methods and environments to take into account the safety, comfort and productivity of human users. It might sound rather grand when applied to the business of organizing your office space, but there is no doubt that the choice and positioning of furniture, equipment, reference material and accessories can have a major impact on the way you work.

furniture

desks

Your desk needs sufficient clear space for you to be able to work comfortably and without distraction. We will come onto clearing the clutter a little later. If you have to divide your time between computer and paperwork, consider a modern wrap-around style which allows you to move between a traditional desktop and computer workstation without getting up. If you have any choice in the matter, go for a desk with adjustable height settings. Consider how the desk is placed in relation to your office space as a whole. Positioning your desk so that it forms a barrier between you and any visitor creates psychological distance. This may be the effect you want to create, but think about moving it if you want to give a more accessible impression. A desk which faces a wall may offer access to handy space for shelves, pinboards etc. For those working in open-plan offices, facing a wall or screen serves to minimize distractions and casual interruptions.

chairs

Most modern office chairs are designed with castors and swivel action, allowing you to move easily to different parts of your workstation, and providing good back support to prevent fatigue. Reject those which are a triumph of ostentation over ergonomics, and signal more about your position in the organization than your productivity.

There is no such thing as an ideal chair for everybody, but there are certain features you should look for:

- adjustable seat height;
- a backrest which is adjustable both vertically and in a forward-backward direction;
- seat depth which is sufficient if you are tall but not too great if you are short;
- adequate stability;
- castors, if required, which are appropriate for the type of flooring in your office.

---

adjusting your chair

Chair adjustment has to take account of your own body dimensions and the height of your work surface, if this is not adjustable. The general recommendation is that the seat height should be adjusted so that you can sit comfortably with your feet flat on the floor and approximately 5 centimetres clearance between the front of the chair and your calves. Then adjust the backrest up and down as well as forwards and backwards so that it fits comfortably in the hollow of your lower back when you are in a relaxed upright position. If armrests are fitted, their height should be adjusted to the point that they barely touch the underside of your elbows when they are bent at an angle of 90 degrees. Armrests should not lift your elbows at all, and you should remove them if they stop you from sitting close enough to your work surface (Figure 6.1).

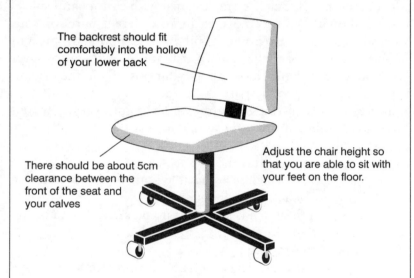

The backrest should fit comfortably into the hollow of your lower back

There should be about 5cm clearance between the front of the seat and your calves

Adjust the chair height so that you are able to sit with your feet on the floor.

Figure 6.1   *Chair adjustment*

So far so good, but the adjustment of your chair also needs to take account of your work surface and keyboard height. You should be able to fit your legs comfortably under the work surface and move them freely. If you can't, the work surface is too low for you and should be adjusted (if possible) or changed. If the work surface is significantly higher than elbow height when you are sitting in your chair, you may need to raise the chair height and use a footrest to maintain a comfortable and safe sitting position.

other furniture

If your office has space for receiving visitors or holding small meetings, give thought to the sort of furniture it contains. Many people still opt for low chairs and a coffee table, but while these create a comfortable and relaxed atmosphere, they are not ideal for doing business. A circular or oval table and upright upholstered chairs is generally preferable for businesslike face-to-face communication without the need to balance papers on your lap.

equipment

I used to know a secretary who was very well organized. She knew exactly where to find everything she needed, and her workstation was neatness itself. When I knew her she had been working for a new boss for about six months. Her previous boss had tended not to use a dictation machine, and she kept her transcription equipment in a box on the top of a high cabinet. The new boss provided her with a daily tape of dictation. So each morning she would clamber up to get her transcription machine out of its box and at the end of each day she would clamber up and put it back.

An extreme example? Certainly, but it serves to illustrate how easy it is for us to leave old work routines in place long after the job has changed. Look at where you keep those items of equipment and accessories that you use regularly. They should be immediately to hand when you need them. If you have shelves above your desk, it should be possible to reach the items on the lowest one without standing up. Avoid placing items you use regularly – telephone, printer, reference books – in positions where you will need to stretch and twist in order to use them.

lighting

Many of the lighting problems in modern offices are associated with computer use, but it is important to have the right sort of lighting conditions for other activities too. Diffusers on overhead lights and the use of desk lamps can help to provide more comfortable conditions for reading and working with printed material. Needless to say, a regular eyesight test is to be recommended. People who have not previously required any vision correction commonly find that by their mid-forties they are having difficulty focusing on close objects, particularly in poor light. Where previously you had to search around for missing papers, now you have to search for your reading glasses before you are able to tell whether you have found your missing papers.

use of the computer

Guidelines for the safe and comfortable use of computers have tended in the past to be targeted primarily at those seen as heavyweight users – data input staff, secretaries, programmers – but so many jobs now involve sustained computer work that all users would be wise to pay attention to them. Taking some simple steps can enhance your productivity, increase your comfort and protect against injury and fatigue.

Here is a basic checklist to follow:

- The normal recommendation is for the top of the monitor screen to be at eye level, although some experts point out that this is the highest it should be, and maintain that for some users a slightly lower monitor proves more comfortable for the eyes and neck.
- Sit with a comfortable and balanced posture, paying particular attention to the position of your neck, spine, elbows, wrists, thighs and feet.
- Don't remain in one position for lengthy periods.
- Keep the forearms, wrists and hands in a straight line and don't rest them on sharp edges. Don't hit the keyboard too hard.

▓ The keyboard should be at the same angle as the fore-arms.

▓ Take frequent breaks from computer activity. Experts suggest five to ten minutes every hour.

▓ Rest your eyes every 10 or 15 minutes by closing them momentarily, gazing at a distant object and blinking frequently.

▓ Position monitors so that light is not reflected off them. Use blinds, diffusers on overhead lighting and anti-glare filters where necessary.

▓ Reading paper documents generally requires better illumination than reading computer screens. If you are working with paper and computer simultaneously, an adjustable desk light can provide additional light on the paper without casting a glare on the computer screen.

▓ A copyholder, either of the free-standing variety or the type which fixes to the side of your monitor, will make it easier for you to view any notes or documents you are using while working on the computer.

▓ Adjust the contrast and brightness on your computer screen to a comfortable level.

▓ Clean the computer screen and other surfaces regularly.

tackle disorganized workspace

Disorganized workspace is a potent source of wasted time and unnecessary stress. Tackling it is a tangible commitment to a more effective way of working. The area on and around your desk is the most important part of your working environment, and you might be tempted to tackle it first. But I suggest that you begin by clearing cupboards and drawers, in order to free up space to accommodate items that are cluttering your immediate desk area.

organizing cupboards, drawers and bookcases

These are all handy hiding places for things you don't need. Start by looking at the cupboards furthest away from your desk – they are likely to have the greatest proportion of redundant material, untouched by previous purges – and move inwards towards your desk. That way you will always have space to house items that are currently jamming up more immediate working areas. Clear out the junk ruthlessly. If there are items that really cannot be discarded, but hardly ever need to be looked at, put them in archive boxes for transfer to central storage, assuming your workplace has such a facility. Remember to take a note of the box contents and file it where you will be able to find it.

Work through all your cupboards and drawers discarding junk, grouping like items together and making sure that items such as box files are clearly labelled. With bookcases it helps to take everything out before rearranging according to subject matter. The fact that books come in stubbornly different sizes means that you won't be able to achieve perfect organization, and you shouldn't waste time trying. All you are attempting to do is organize material so that you can quickly put your hand on it when the need arises.

organizing your desk space

I used to pretend that I could work well with a cluttered desk. Despite the various piles of paper, at times threatening to engulf the workspace, I claimed that I could easily put my hand on any document I needed and that shifting my attention from one task to another kept me sharp throughout my working day. It was nonsense, of course. Superfluous papers are a distraction from the job in hand in much the same way as interruptions and phone calls. It is all too easy to flit around a crowded desk, pecking at tasks rather than devoting the concentrated effort needed to complete them. The presence of a multiplicity of documents is also an excuse for procrastination. When you are struggling with one task, it's the most simple thing in the world to shift your energy and attention to another, seemingly more straightforward chore which beckons from the top of a nearby pile.

Searching for documents can waste considerable amounts of time and throw up further distractions. Just consider the number of times you need to root through the piles when a request or phone call summons the presence of a particular piece of paper. Surveys have suggested that 15 minutes a day is a fairly conservative estimate. It doesn't sound much, does it? But when you consider that 15 minutes a day is equal to a week and a half out of every year, the waste of your time is much more apparent. What could you do with that time? If you are disorganized to the extent that you spend 30 minutes a day searching for things, then the reward for greater discipline could be almost three weeks of additional productive activity.

Desktop disorganization also destroys your ability to set priorities. Within the same pile there are likely to be scribbled notes, half-drafted reports, important letters and complete junk. All share a common fate – their importance is only considered when they come to the top of the pile or force themselves on your consciousness in the course of a search for something else.

And then there is the sheer inefficiency of it all. When you start a new task you have to clear some working space, pushing previously incomplete activity into yet higher piles. The same items pass through your hands numerous times, surfacing and resurfacing from the confusion of papers. You waste energy on things that should have been discarded the very first time you saw them. You miss deadlines because the papers that would remind you of them are buried under heaps of other stuff. You even find yourself sorting through the waste paper basket for that important piece of information you remember scribbling on a scrap of paper, which might have been the one which made no sense to you when you picked it out of the pile this morning.

Finally there is the stress. All the time that your untackled paperwork is an amorphous mass, it represents a potent source of disquiet. You are not entirely sure what lurks within those piles and they remain an ever-present reminder of your failure to get on top of your job. Very often the presence of tasks to be done is more stressful than actually doing them.

So are you convinced? Sure. All that remains now is to do something about it. Simplicity has to be the keynote of your desk organization. One of everything is a good place to start – one in tray, one out tray, one diary, one notebook. Think about whether you need personal clutter around your desktop. You may want to keep the odd photo or memento but there should be no sense in which personal reminders impose on your ability to work effectively. Accessories and equipment on your desktop should consist of items that you use daily. Other things may be kept close to hand but away from your main working surface. Give yourself plenty of space to work. There is a psychological advantage to the absence of clutter as well as a physical one.

You may need to overcome a mental hurdle in clearing your desk. There is a tendency to associate the crowded desk with a busy owner, and we like to think of ourselves as busy. Remember, however, that one can be busy but incompetent and unproductive. Let the results of your activities speak for you rather than the appearance of your desk. Once you are clear about what has a place on your desk, you are ready to tackle the piles.

get rid of the piles

The prospect of tackling the piles of paper which have built up on your desk and around your office may be intimidating but, by setting aside some time for a disciplined blitz, you can get rid of them and lift the mental weight of their presence. In addition to items which need action on your part or should be directed to others, it is likely that your paper piles will consist of documents (reports, periodicals etc) which you have put aside to be read later, items which have not made it to the filing cabinet, and things which you were not sure what to do with.

Your objective is to get through the paper piles; you must not let yourself become bogged down. So, be prepared to attack the offending heaps and deal quickly and decisively with their contents (Figure 6.2):

■ Earmark four empty folders, filing trays or baskets and mark them: Deal with, Distribute, Read, File. Make sure you have sufficient plastic bin bags for the most important category – the discard pile.

■ Approach the task with the view that the majority of items are destined for the bin. Whatever relevance they had when they joined the pile is likely to have diminished. Don't repeat previous indecisiveness. If in doubt, throw it out.

■ Don't waste time reading items. Skim them to the point of determining whether they are needed and if so put them in the relevant tray or basket.

■ Don't file or act upon things as you go; you will become bogged down and distracted. By all means mark items to assist your actions and filing later, but keep to your main objective – to blast through the pile.

■ Zip through magazines and periodicals, tearing out the pages containing articles you wish to keep and throwing the rest away. Don't stop to read any of them at this stage.

■ When you have worked your way through the piles, turn your attention to the four trays. Schedule time to deal with the reading and filing tasks, and use your 'bring forward' system to determine when the 'deal with' items will be actioned.

Tackled in this way, a fearsome chore can become a real stress buster.

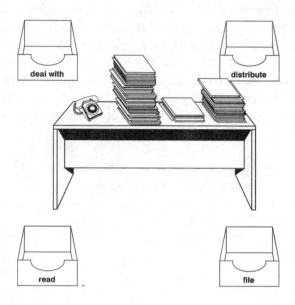

Figure 6.2   *Get rid of the piles*

keeping things that way

OK, so you've managed to sort the contents of your office. The things you use regularly are close at hand, you have ditched the junk and cleared the piles. How do you keep it that way?

The answer is, I'm afraid, a boring one. It has a lot to do with developing positive work habits:

■ Move paperwork quickly in line with the five Ds outlined in Chapter 4.
■ If in doubt throw it out!
■ Don't use your desk as filing space – use project folders or 'bring forward' files for work in progress (see Chapter 7).

▓ Keep your equipment needs under review. Are the items you use regularly still in the most accessible places?

▓ Don't transfer piles of paper on your desk to piles of paper in other parts of the office.

▓ Try to file on a daily basis. When you remove items from your filing cabinets, make a practice of re-filing them as soon as possible.

summary

The key aspects of organizing your workspace are:

▓ arranging your furniture and equipment to maximize safety, comfort and productivity;

▓ freeing up time and space by reorganizing your desk and storage space;

▓ reducing stress by eliminating stacks of paper around your office.

organize filing systems

No aspect of personal organization attracts more shudders than filing. But for all that we loathe it, we seldom stop to consider why we are doing it. The only reason for putting a document into a file is so that you can find it easily. And the only reason that you might want to do that is to help you fulfil some aspect of your job in the future.

Get rid of the quasi-religious aspects of filing – eternal damnation will be visited on those whose files are not well stuffed. Files are a resource for your use, simple as that. You should be the one who benefits from them, so you need to make them work for you.

Up to 85 per cent of the material stored in the average filing cabinet is never referred to again. That means, for every five documents painstakingly categorized, punched and filed, only one will be needed in the future. And the chances are that the one that is needed will prove frustratingly difficult to locate. It's a case of the 85 per cent you don't need getting in the way of the 15 per cent that you do.

You can never predict with certainty those documents you will need again. Some things do need to be stored on a 'just in case' basis, but you can drastically cut down on the chore of filing and failure to find the documents you need by more confident use of the 'discard' option when you first receive material. Filing is not a matter of getting a document off your desk when you're frightened to throw it away, but are not sure what else to do with it. A document should only make it to the filing cabinet when it cannot be readily accessed elsewhere and there is a reasonable chance that it will be needed again in the future.

If you can step away from a defensive filing mentality – better save it, just in case – to an attacking frame of mind, then you have much more chance of getting yourself a lean, mean filing system that works for you. For every document you consider filing, ask yourself, 'What use will this document be to me in the future?' If you don't get a convincing answer, ditch it.

In addition to defensive filing, there are a number of other common document storage problems. How many of the following apply to you:

- inappropriately located information?
- no structure to the filing system?
- a structure which hasn't been kept to?
- insufficient thought given to the appropriate grouping of items to allow for easy retrieval?
- failure to weed out obsolete material?
- forgetting what files you already have and setting up folders which duplicate existing categories of information?
- filing material that is easily accessible elsewhere?
- setting up too many categories within a system so that it becomes unmanageable?
- use of inappropriate storage equipment for particular types of material (eg suspended files straining to hold weighty reports and periodicals)?
- time spent searching for things which have been misfiled?

▦ indecision about where to put things?
▦ missing files that have been 'borrowed' by person or persons unknown?

locate information appropriately

Your choice of location and storage medium should take account of the frequency with which you may need to consult files.

current projects and activities

These are files which you may need to consult several times in the course of a day and so should be kept either in desk filing drawers or a filing cart immediately next to your desk. As well as files for individual projects or assignments in progress, you may want to earmark a file each for correspondence pending, reading and meetings. They can help you to avoid the tendency to put things back into your in tray or to create piles on your desk. If you choose this approach, you need to take care that these files don't become general dumping areas. 'To read' files are particularly prone to this. General files may also result in date-related information being overlooked – preparatory reading for a meeting, for example, or a letter which needs to be answered by a particular date. Use a concertina file with a 'bring forward' system (see Chapter 4) to overcome this problem.

main reference files

Your main filing system is for the things you need to refer to from time to time. Material from the current projects and activities category will find its way there provided it is worth keeping. Don't simply transfer current project files to your main filing cabinet when the project is completed. Very often they will be cluttered with working papers and rough drafts that are of no further significance. Ruthlessly weed out the junk if you want to be able to lay your hands on the important stuff.

setting up your filing system

First decide on broad divisions in which you want to group your files. These will clearly depend on the nature of your work, but examples of category titles might include: personnel, customers, projects or administration. You might like to consider colour coding files within each category, so that when seeking a file you can quickly go to the right part of the cabinet. This is particularly useful when you are using a lateral filing system rather than a drawer filing cabinet. Alphabetical order is normally the most convenient arrangement for individual files within a category.

In deciding the titles for individual files, choose the broadest possible description consistent with manageability. You will want to avoid the need to split overlarge files within a short time and, equally, will not want to find yourself with lots of files each containing just a few documents. Neither is conducive to easy retrieval, which is the sole reason you are engaged in the task. If your file headings are too broad, then you might as well leave the documents in piles. Don't try to predict all the files you may need in the future – you'll end up with some empty folders if you do – but remember that your system needs the capacity to expand rationally, so allow space within files and sections for it to do so. Keep titles short and simple, and try to avoid descriptions that are vague or woolly. Miscellaneous files are notorious black holes.

Choose storage which is appropriate for the material. Use magazine files or box files rather than hanging folders for bulky reports and periodicals. Consider whether you need to store complete copies of magazines and periodicals. Cuttings take up far less room and it is much easier to find the item you want.

filing documents

If you are following the paper handling procedures recommended in Chapter 4, you will already have weeded out that which isn't worth keeping. Here are some additional pointers to ensure that your paper storage is as effectively managed as possible:

■ Make a note indicating the intended destination file at the top of any document you have decided to file. This prevents you having to reread and decide on destination when you actually come to file the document.

■ If you are uncertain about where to put an item, think about the most likely context in which you are liable to require it in the future.

■ Keep a list of your files handy to help refresh your memory when deciding where to file an item, and to avoid opening new files which overlap with those that already exist.

■ Don't file hard copy of information already stored on computer. Ensure a sensible directory structure for your computer files with reliable back-up. It is quicker to do, easier to find and amend, and takes up less room.

■ Don't file material which is readily available from other sources such as the originator of the document, central archives, Internet reference sources.

■ Build up a filing habit. Spending a little time regularly is much less of a chore than trying to wade through a large pile of documents for filing. Try to file daily if possible.

■ If you are tempted to file an item you haven't been bothered to read, ask yourself a very serious 'Why?'

■ If missing files are a problem in your office, a simple tracking system can be introduced. Keep some A4 cards by the filing cabinets, each divided into three columns: Name, Location, Date. Anybody borrowing a file enters their details on the card and places it in the appropriate empty file pocket.

If somebody else does your filing for you, it is tempting to leave the whole tedious business to them. But remember that it is still your information, and it is worthwhile knowing the structure of the filing system so that when you mark a document for filing you are sending it to a known location rather than to a black hole. This process of mentally slotting the document into place will assist your memory of its existence.

pruning and weeding your files

Without regular attention, files can rapidly become out of hand. The storage life of material varies hugely according to the nature of the information. Some items become redundant in a matter of weeks while others need to be kept for years. Weeding out what needs to be discarded or archived can be daunting. If you are working with a file and notice that it contains obsolete information, weed it out there and then, but don't let yourself be distracted from your current task into a lengthy sorting process.

Try to schedule a regular file overhaul. You may opt either for 'big bang' or for 'little and often'. The former is a trawl through all your files, say, every three months. The latter might mean spending five or ten minutes sorting a couple of files at the end of each day. Both have drawbacks. If you're over-loaded, and who isn't these days, the big bang tends to get post-poned indefinitely until a very serious problem builds up. Little and often requires some attention to building up a habit.

However you set about the task, you need to be ruthless with the rubbish and not to allow yourself to become bogged down in spin-off tasks. If there are items which have been misplaced, or one file needs to be merged with another, just put the items where they need to go, and resist the temptation to sort the destination file unless it is one you have already dealt with. Its turn will come in due course.

electronic filing of paper documents

Organizations are increasingly using shared document storage, often in an electronic form. These have the advantage of saving much of the time and space occupied by traditional filing methods, as well as greatly facilitating retrieval of documents.

Company-wide document systems are outside the scope of this book, but it is now inexpensive and easy to use these methods with a standard PC for small-scale and personal filing systems. In addition to the computer, you need appropriate software and two hardware elements: a means of getting documents into the computer (scanner), and a large capacity storage device such as a writable CD ROM drive. Such devices now retail very cheaply, and frequently come with free document-filing software. CDs can store large quantities of material and, with the rewritable variety, it is possible to store and delete information many times over almost as simply as using a floppy disk (Figure 7.1).

Some software will allow you to store all types of electronic files together – scanned documents, word-processor and spreadsheet files, and e-mails or documents downloaded from the Internet. All may be accessed in a flash using subject category, keywords or date filed. Remember, however, that putting paper documents into the system still takes time, and so you should not use an electronic filing system as an excuse for abandoning any discrimination about what gets filed and what thrown away.

document input   processing   storage

scanner   PC with appropriate software   writable CD-ROM

Figure 7.1 *A small-scale document storage system*

Don't use the scanner for documents which have been originated on your own computer. Documents which have been
scanned are stored in a compressed image form which uses a lot
more storage space than a word-processed file of equivalent
length. If you put word-processed documents back into the
computer in this way, you are likely to find your CD filling up
more quickly than you would wish.

organizing computer files

The basic principles of organizing your computer files are
really no different from those for the paper variety. You want a
simple and logical grouping of material which ensures minimal
time and hassle spent looking for files at a later date. It's true
that the search facilities on your computer greatly reduce the
incidence of files becoming hopelessly buried, as they so easily
can in a traditional filing system, but you don't want to be
reduced to running a search every time you need to recall a
document. A logical arrangement of folders, sub-folders and

file names will allow you to go quickly to the document you require:

1. Decide what will be your first-level document storage folder. My preferred way of working is to create a new main folder for each year. It allows for easy archiving and prevents sub-folders of routine documents becoming out of hand.
2. Within your main folder, set up sub-folders for the different types of routine document you create. Depending on the precise nature of your work, you might choose: letters, minutes, memos, reports, etc. Set up sub-folders also for any major projects which will require the creation of documents or spreadsheets. (In my folder for 1999 there is a sub-folder for this book.)
3. Inform your computer applications where to put things. When you click on the 'Open' or 'Save' command, you want the computer to go to your first-level storage folder (eg 1999) and you may need to change the existing settings so that it does so. Such changes are generally made by clicking onto the 'Options' or 'Preferences' command within your application's 'Tools' menu. If you are using Microsoft Word, for example, you go to 'Tools' then 'Options', click on the 'File Locations' tab, and then modify the file location for your documents.

choosing file names

It's all about simplicity and accessibility once again. You need file names that will mean something to you when you seek them out. You don't want the irritation and time-waste of opening a file only to find that it is not what you thought it was. If your software automatically offers a file name based on the heading you have used for the document, this may be quite adequate, but take care if you are producing a number of documents which have similar headings. Documents such as letters, minutes and memos are best saved with a name and a date (Bloggs 15–12 or Safety 30–6) so that other documents relating to the same person or meeting can easily be identified. The limitations of MSDOS and Windows operating systems prior to Windows 95 meant that file names could not exceed eight characters. If you have changed from one of these older operating systems fairly recently, you may be locked into habits of file name abbreviation that are no longer necessary.

back-up

With computer-based information, unlike paper, you don't need to be so rigorous about what to save and what to discard, but you do need to devote attention to back-up. Few office experiences can be more stressful than the complete loss of days, weeks or months of work with no prospect of recovering it. And yet, for all that back-up is a quick and straightforward process, it is remarkable how many competent computer users fail to carry it out regularly enough.

what do you back up?

It is unlikely that you will want to back up everything on your system. If a crash occurs, applications can be re-installed. The files you have created are the ones which must be backed up, and they tend not to take up a great deal of space. Identify the locations of your key data files – word processor documents, spreadsheet files, database files, personal information manager files etc. Use Windows Backup or other software to keep track of the important files and folders, so that they can be backed up in one simple operation without the need to identify them afresh every time.

where to back up

There are now a host of media you can use for back-up. The floppy disk is old technology but still has a role to play where limited quantities of data are concerned. Larger volume storage devices, such as zip drives or CD-ROM, are now very cheap and simple to use. If you are connected to a network, there may be a facility for back-up onto a network drive. The most important consideration is that you should not be backing up onto the same hard drive that contains your original files, and if there is any danger of theft, the place that you store your back-up information should be separate from your PC. The ultimate back-up location is now being offered by some Internet sites which, for a small fee, will provide you with secure storage space in a remote location via the Internet. The theory is that you are then safe from every conceivable catastrophe – computer crash, fire, theft, earthquake – everything except forgetting your password.

summary

Effective storage of information requires:

- clarity about what is and is not worth filing;
- a simple and logical structure which is routinely adhered to;
- choice of meaningful file names and category titles;
- regular pruning of redundant material;
- frequent reliable back-up of electronic information.

use technology to assist

Technology may be both an aid to organization and a factor leading to greater disorganization. Technologically assisted generation and communication of information has led to a huge increase in the volume of information in daily circulation, and far from achieving the paperless office envisaged in the early 1980s, ever larger quantities of paper are being produced, handled and stored. Add to that the increasing use of e-mail and the biggest information repository of all, the Internet, and you have a recipe for overload. But the tremendous capacity of technology to assist us in creating, communicating, manipulating and storing information also offers potential solutions to the problem. Your success in this will depend on judicious choice and effective use of the available tools.

know when not to use technology

Information technology has become so all pervading that one may be tempted to use it for every information handling task.

This would be a mistake. There are occasions when the effort of using technology outweighs the advantage, or the medium is inappropriate:

▦ producing a word-processed memo in response to an internal communication, when a simple hand-written note on the original document would suffice;

▦ setting up a computer database of contact phone numbers when your number of contacts is limited and likely to stay that way;

▦ using time and energy to learn a software package to carry out a function that could be performed manually and has only marginal or occasional significance in your workload.

choose appropriate software

Let genuine needs drive your software decisions. It is all too easy to be enticed by the productivity claims of a particular software package, and having acquired it, to look around for a task on which to use it. Using a product to meet an identified need is generally an effective way of learning it, but take care not to set yourself unrealistic timescales for achieving your targets with a new application.

Match the pay-off in terms of improved productivity against the investment of time to become proficient in the application. Even if a package looks straightforward, allow plenty of time to get to grips with it. There may be unexpected glitches to overcome.

The value of a particular package will vary from person to person. It will be dependent on how much you have used other similar products, the way you like to work and the precise nature of your job. Use magazine reviews and recommendations to aid your decision, but recognize that only you can make an accurate assessment of whether an application is worth having.

if you are new to computers

If you are new to computers, you should go initially for the easiest to learn general software without attempting to analyse your needs too deeply. You are likely to get the greatest personal organization advantage by learning to use a personal information manager, e-mail and a word processor.

The most common problems for new computer users are not knowing where to start, and fear of making disastrous mistakes. The first is a matter of taking one's courage in both hands and pitching in. To the novice, everything may seem daunting, but each step forward makes the next one less difficult. Many computer operations have the same basic format. There are a host of good tutorials in book form or CD ROM. Once you have mastered the basics, nothing can beat tackling a real project for reinforcing and progressing your learning.

Conquering fear of making mistakes starts with the understanding that there is almost nothing irretrievable you can do from the keyboard, short of pouring coffee into it. Take care to save your work regularly and even seemingly catastrophic situations can be salvaged. It is helpful if there is somebody experienced to call upon when the unpredictable does happen, as it surely will. There is usually a simple and easily executed solution. If you don't have expert assistance, resist the temptation to express anger, and approach the difficulty methodically, making use of the troubleshooting section in your software manual or the help facility within the application.

Don't try to learn too much at once. Get to grips with one package before moving on to the next. The majority of software is now based on Microsoft Windows and has very similar screen layout and commands. If you have mastered one package, you can easily transfer to the next your knowledge of the familiar features, and work to address those aspects that are different.

if you are an experienced computer user

Before embarking on a new application, try to arrive at a realistic assessment of the benefits set against the investment of time in learning to use it. One way to do this is to estimate a payback period. The questions to ask yourself are:

- What will I use this package for?
- How much time per week do I currently spend doing these tasks?
- What are the weekly time savings I might reasonably expect once I am a competent user of the package?
- How many learning hours will it take for me to achieve reasonable competence?

If you then divide the learning hours estimate by the figure for weekly time savings, you will arrive at an estimated payback period. For example, if it takes you 20 hours to learn a package that only saves you 30 minutes a week, the payback period will be 40 weeks. In other words, it will be almost a year before you derive any time saving. In this situation, there are likely to be other time investments which will produce more immediate rewards.

deciding to upgrade

Whatever software package you choose, within a short time there is likely to be an upgrade version available, promising new features and greater effectiveness. Make the decision on whether to upgrade on the following basis:

Do I need the new features? Few of us use all the features of an application. New ones may sound attractive, but if they don't offer you significant benefits there is no point in acquiring them. *Are the advantages worth the learning investment?* Most upgraded packages will be broadly similar to their predecessors, but sometimes there is a major redesign which will require you to 'relearn' the application. Against this, the improvements may only be marginal. An upgrade may, from time to time, introduce new bugs or frustrations, or may run more slowly on your computer.

reviewing computer habits

The longer you have been using computers, the more likely it is that you will benefit from a review of your computer habits. Experienced users may find that they are locked into ways of doing things which were learnt when computers were slower and software less sophisticated; or that the trial and error way in which learning took place has bypassed important shortcuts. Half an hour revisiting the help file or manual of a software package or operating system may pay major dividends. Here are some of the things you might look for:

- facilities which weren't present in earlier versions of applications or operating systems;
- keyboard shortcuts on commonly used commands;
- drag and drop procedures to replace lengthy operations;
- full use of available templates;
- automatic functions – auto-correct, auto-fill;
- customization of toolbars and menus.

useful tools

Some tools to assist with organization – eg PIMs and electronic filing – have already been discussed. In the section that follows I will briefly consider some other applications which may be of assistance in organizing your working life. I will limit consideration to those that are of fairly general applicability. Use of the Internet and e-mail communication will be covered in Chapter 9.

word processors

The word processor is the ubiquitous computer application and one of the simplest with which to be up and running quickly. Provided that you can navigate the keyboard, use the 'delete' and 'backspace' keys and the 'save' and 'print' functions, you can use the word processor at a basic level to create, store and amend documents. To produce attractive documents you will need to use some of the layout functions, but the standard templates which come with most word processors can do most of the work for you. In recent years, word processors have developed greatly in both sophistication and ease of use. They offer a multiplicity of tools which the average user does not employ, such as the ability to incorporate pictures, charts and tables into documents, to perform calculations and to display revisions.

Do I need to use a word processor if I already have secretarial assistance?
The answer to this depends on the way you like to work. Many people find that they can rapidly dictate routine items, but need to see more complex material in print as they develop it. If this applies to you, then you may benefit from structuring your thoughts on the word processor. Most word processors have an outlining facility which allows you to build up your

structure from headings and sub-headings. You may wish to put the draft of a document together and then leave your secretary to work on layout and graphics. Alternatively, you may wish to type the more complex passages and dictate the rest.

spreadsheets

Spreadsheets can store and manipulate any form of numerical information. If you have to keep track and make sense of financial or statistical data, then some time spent learning a spreadsheet package may be valuable. In recent years, spreadsheet software designers have made it much easier for the average user to perform quite complex calculations. Charts and graphs can be generated from spreadsheet data with a couple of mouse clicks. However, most new users will find spreadsheets a little trickier to learn than word processors.

project management software

Specialist project management software such as Microsoft Project is very powerful and is capable of allocating and tracking tasks and resources across several complex projects simultaneously. If you are going to make full use of such facilities, you will benefit from some knowledge of project management conventions, and you will need to spend a significant amount of time learning the product. There are other more basic programs available, including some quite good packages which can be downloaded from the Internet. If you simply want to track personal projects and assignments for a small number of other people, you may well find that the scheduling facilities of a Personal Information Manager will be adequate for your needs.

voice recognition software

With a voice recognition package, you can dictate material via a microphone and the computer will convert your speech into text. There are a number of products available. Early packages required the separate enunciation of each word in a manner which is difficult to achieve when speaking naturally. However, the software has developed to a point where it can now cope with normal speech, and producers claim up to 98 per cent accuracy with speeds up to 160 words per minute. Some packages come with a digital dictation machine which allows you to feed recorded material directly into your computer and have it converted to text. To make use of a voice recognition package, your computer will need a reasonably fast processor and plenty of memory. Check the minimum specifications carefully before buying and confirm that the package will work with the word-processing or other software with which you want to use it. You should be prepared to spend some time 'training' the package to recognize your particular speech patterns and correcting a significant number of mistakes which will occur before the package becomes used to your voice.

presentation software

If you frequently have presentations to make, software such as Microsoft PowerPoint or Corel Presentations will not only save you preparation time, but will greatly enhance impact. These applications are very quick and easy to get to grips with. They offer an outline view which is useful for shaping up your thoughts prior to formatting the presentation slides. There are templates that can remove much of the donkey work from standard presentations, and it is a simple matter to import tables from your word processor, charts from your spreadsheet or graphics from other programs. Editing the presentation and preparing accompanying notes are also extremely easy, as is the copying of material from one presentation to another. In addition, there is the opportunity to add sound and animation effects or to design hidden slides which can be revealed when needed – in responses to questions, for example.

To make full use of presentation software, you need some means of displaying the presentation on a screen large enough for all your audience to see easily. If your audience consists of no more than three or four people, a standard computer screen may be large enough. For slightly larger groups, a PC to TV connection or adaptor will do. Otherwise, unless you are operating in an environment which has a permanently wired conference display screen, you will need either an overhead projector tablet or a multimedia projector. Until recently, projectors were bulky and expensive, but they are now coming down in size and price. A few computer suppliers produce a laptop model with a screen that can be converted to an overhead projector tablet by removing a back panel. This saves both the cost and additional weight of a separate display tablet, but you will still need an overhead projector to display it on.

desktop publishing software

DTP packages have become less prominent in general use as the sophistication of word processors has increased, but they still have a distinct edge on tasks that require attractive presentation of text and graphics in such things as brochures, newsletters and advertisements. At the top end of the range are the professional products such as Quark Express and Adobe PageMaker which are powerful and rather pricey. But there are a number of inexpensive DTP packages like Microsoft Publisher, Serif Page Plus, and GST Power Publisher which combine ease of use with the capacity for sophisticated output. What many general users forget, however, is that design flair and skill are at least as important as the ability to use the software. Standard templates can help overcome our design deficiencies, but if you are tempted to use DTP software yourself to produce materials which need to have an impact, ask yourself honestly whether the product of your effort is likely to do justice to the organization you work for and the investment of your time. Contracting this sort of work out is not normally expensive.

databases

The term 'database' covers a vast range of applications which have the function of storing and manipulating information. Many of these are pre-formatted for a particular purpose (eg PIMs) or written to meet a particular company's requirements, and our interaction with them will consist of inputting and extracting data. General 'blank sheet' databases, such as Microsoft Access and Lotus Approach are standard components of integrated office suites and are included here for that reason. They are extremely powerful tools which can greatly assist office organization. But the value of the average user learning the skills to set up a database, as opposed to entering and extracting information from one that somebody else has set up, is debatable. For most of us there will never be a need to set up more than one or two databases and the learning investment will not be repaid. Generally, you will be better off adapting a pre-formatted database to your needs – there are a host of companies offering ready formatted packages for standard business functions such as personnel, accounts, job costing etc – or, if something specific is required, getting somebody skilled in database design to produce one for you.

keyboard training packages

If you are a two-finger typist who does a significant amount of keyboard work, you may benefit from the increase in typing speed which follows from developing the use of all your fingers. There are a number of inexpensive keyboard trainers available on CD-ROM which take you through staged development and practice. It is not unreasonable to look for a doubling of your speed with eight to twelve hours of work. If you have been typing with two fingers for a long time, then you might find it a little more difficult to make the change, but as a former two-finger typist of 30 years standing, I can testify that the change is possible with a little perseverance, and makes a considerable difference to productivity.

using voicemail

Few aspects of modern office technology can be more universally hated than voicemail. Callers, who may have already negotiated their way through a selection of number press options, find themselves dealing, not with a human being, but with a poorly recorded message complete with background babble. For the voicemail recipient there are interruptions to other work as the software periodically rings to notify them of messages received followed by the need to replay rambling and inaudible messages in an attempt to capture crucial information.

For all that, voicemail is certainly here to stay and it can assist your personal organization provided that you use it properly. The most important aspect of voicemail should be its time independence – it should not be allowed to become an interruption to other tasks. If the system is set up for your phone to ring at predetermined intervals to deliver your voicemail messages, disable this facility if possible. It may just require the entry of a standard code. Failing this, set your voicemail to receive messages and turn off the ringing tone or physically unplug the phone. Collect your voicemail messages when you are ready to deal with them.

Recognize that voicemail is an essential part of your personal presentation and invest in it the same vitality and efficiency that you would hope to bring to your face-to-face dealings. Here are some tips.

recording your message

▨ Keep your outgoing message brief and lively. Check it for audibility and energy after you have recorded it.

■ Change your message to let callers know if you are going to be away from the office for more than a day. This will prevent repeat calls and duplicate messages. Remember to revert to the original message when you return.

■ Consider giving an alternative contact number if you will be unable to deal with messages for a while.

■ Make a point of returning messages within a reasonable time of receiving them.

leaving messages for others

■ Keep your messages brief and to the point.

■ If voicemail catches you by surprise and you have a complex message to deliver, hang up and take a few moments to collect your thoughts before phoning again, rather than leaving a vague and rambling message. This said, it pays to note beforehand the points you wish to cover when embarking on any complex or potentially difficult phone conversation.

■ Enunciate your phone number clearly at the beginning and end of the message and spell any words that will be unfamiliar to the recipient.

summary

Modern information technology can be of considerable assistance in personal organization provided it is used appropriately. You need to:

■ recognize the tasks for which technology offers no advantage;

■ select software to meet identified needs;

■ balance potential time savings against the commitment of time to learn new software applications;

■ review your computer habits periodically;

■ use voicemail appropriately.

organize your use of the Internet

Whatever other technological tools you choose, there is little chance that you will be able to escape involvement with the Internet. It has already revolutionized communication and access to information, and its role as an everyday vehicle for business is set to continue increasing over the coming years. There is a downside, however. E-mail suffers from the same overload problems as paper communication, with the added dimension that the even greater ease of copying and transmission makes junk mail yet more prevalent. And while the speed and ease with which you are able to access information on the World Wide Web can greatly assist with personal organization, the sheer volume of information available presents several difficulties:

- separating the information you need from the mass of less relevant data;
- deciding when to stop searching;
- avoiding the distraction presented by other interesting but irrelevant material;
- assessing the quality and reliability of information.

In this chapter we will look at how to avoid the potential difficulties and to get the best out of the medium. It is beyond
the scope of this book to provide a detailed introduction for
those wishing to set up an Internet account and use the software for the first time. New users should not, however, be
deterred. The installation of Internet software requires minimal
computer knowledge or user intervention, and packages like
Internet Explorer (Internet browser) and Outlook Express (e-
mail) provide excellent introductions to their facilities. For
anybody requiring more, there are a host of good introductory
books.

e-mail

If you are not already using e-mail for regular business communication, then you probably should be considering it. E-mail is
one of the simplest computer applications to use. Even a
computer novice can master it in an hour or so. It is:

▆ *Immediate.* You can tap out an e-mail message and
deliver it to its destination in moments – no need to
worry about printer access, envelopes or catching the
post. Supporting documents, spreadsheets, drawings,
even video can be sent as attachments, provided the
recipient has the appropriate software to open them.

▆ *Informal.* Forget about letter writing and memo
conventions, with e-mail the basic memo structure is
set up for you, and you don't need to worry about
whether your communication fills the page. Three
words are as acceptable as 300.

▆ *Easy to file or discard.* Provided that you have set up
your system adequately, you can instantly file any e-
mail message that it is important to save. Those that
do not need to be kept are somehow easier to blast

into oblivion by the fact that they do not appear on paper.

E-mail works in a similar fashion whether you are operating within a company network (Intranet) or across the globe (Internet). The software on your own machine communicates with that on a remote computer (either your company network server or the mail server of your Internet service provider) to pass on messages that you wish to despatch and to pick up messages with your mailbox address.

It is important, of course, to have other e-mail users to communicate with. If the majority of your contacts are not yet on e-mail, then you will gain minimal advantage from gearing yourself up to use it. However, this is becoming increasingly unlikely as more and more people and organizations tap into its benefits.

ten tips for effective e-mail use

1. Treat your e-mail in-box in accordance with the recommendations for incoming paper in Chapter 4. Take a positive action with each message when you look at it for the first time (discard, deal with, direct, deposit, determine future action)

2. Don't let incoming e-mail messages become a source of interruption or distraction from the task you are currently engaged upon. Just because it is an immediate communication medium doesn't mean that you have to deal with it immediately. Unlike telephone calls or other interruptions, e-mail messages will sit in your in-box until you are ready to deal with them. Effective e-mail users will make use of this time independence. They will turn off any automatic notification of incoming mail and deal with their messages once or twice a day when other tasks are not a priority.

3. Finding e-mail addresses can be frustrating. There are directories and search facilities, which will look for e-mail addresses, but they are very incomplete as registration of e-mail addresses normally depends on a deliberate voluntary act by individuals. Having to phone somebody to ask for their e-mail address seems to defeat the whole purpose of this slick technology, so make a practice of hanging on to e-mail addresses that you might need to use again. Outlook Express offers a search facility with several online directories and also has the option of automatically capturing the e-mail address of any correspondent to whom you reply.

4. Maintain just one e-mail address for normal use. With the growth of free Internet service providers, there is an increasing tendency to have more than one Internet account, each with its own e-mail facility. While it may be reasonable to maintain one e-mail address for business and another for personal use, more than one address devoted to business use means that you are going to spend time hopping in and out of mailboxes to check mail, and may cause confusion for those with whom you are communicating.

5. The informality of e-mail and the ability to send instant replies can easily lure you into reckless or ill-considered communication. If you are not entirely confident about what you want to say, or a message from somebody has angered you, compose your e-mail response offline and only send it when you are happy about the content. Remember also that the ease with which e-mails can be forwarded may mean that your message finds its way to a destination beyond that which you had originally intended – a potential source of embarrassment for the unwary.

6. Make e-mail subject lines as clear as possible so that it is easy for recipients to understand quickly what

they are about before opening them. A well-drafted subject line can mean that your message is dealt with more quickly.

7. You may find that your word processor, with its more sophisticated text handling capabilities, is more suited than your e-mail software to the preparation of complex messages. Use the word processor and copy the text into the e-mail software when you are satisfied with it. Alternatively, send the word-processed document as an e-mail attachment, provided you are confident that the recipient has a compatible word processor that will enable them to open the document and read it.

8. Don't worry about discarding items unread. If the header information suggests that an item is not worth reading, click the Delete button. Waste no more time. Just one word of warning – some recent e-mail software allows users to specify a 'read receipt'. This sends an automatic message back to the originator when the recipient opens the message to read it. So if you are worried about offending the sender, at least open the message before deleting it.

9. Create suitably indexed folders on your hard drive to store any e-mail messages you wish to keep, so that you can easily find them again.

10. When sending e-mails, indicate if you don't require an answer. Otherwise, people will often respond with just a brief addition to the original message; time wasting for you to open and read.

getting rid of junk e-mail

It is scarcely any more expensive to send an e-mail message to 100 people than to one person. When you consider that sending one e-mail costs but a fraction of sending a letter, you start to see the attractiveness of bulk e-mailings.

There are two types of e-mail you may wish to rid yourself of. The first concerns legitimate bulk mailings that you have signed up for at some stage, but are no longer interested in receiving. Usually you will find that these include a simple response message that you can use to take yourself off the list.

The second type are more pernicious unsolicited mailings which have arisen from your e-mail address being 'harvested' automatically by software which trawls newsgroups and Web sites. This junk mail, known as 'spam', is an increasing problem. Trying to get yourself off the junk e-mailers' lists once you are on them is generally fruitless, and experts recommend a two-part strategy:

- ■ Take steps to limit access to your e-mail address. Don't spread it around unnecessarily. If you post messages to newsgroups, disguise your e-mail address in such a way that it will be recognizable to a human being but not the automatic software that 'harvests' addresses. Thus bill.bloggs@isp.com might become bill.bloggs@ nojunkisp.com.
- ■ Use your e-mail software to filter out unwanted mail There is a facility in Outlook Express by which you can designate e-mail addresses from which you do not wish to receive mail. Whenever the software encounters a message from an unwanted address, it will automatically divert it to your delete box. You can also use this facility to divert messages that have particular words in the subject line. The full version of Outlook goes a step further with more powerful blocking facilities (Figure 9.1).

finding information on the Internet

The Internet is huge and seductively accessible. You are just a

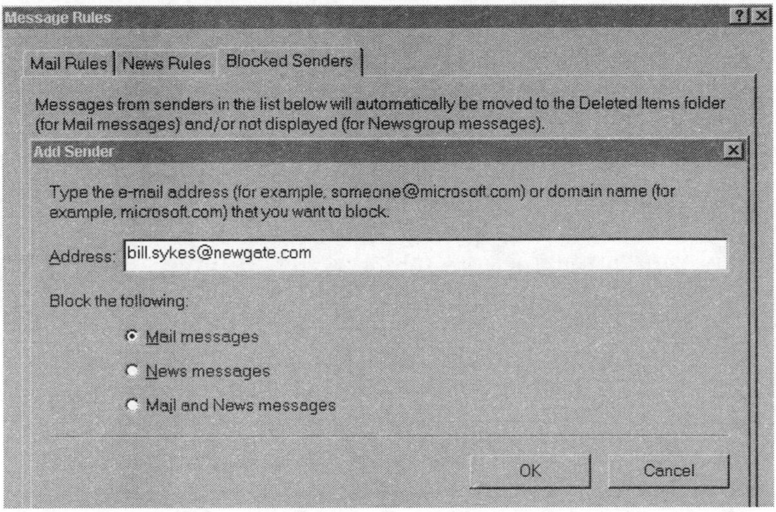

Message Rules ?×

Mail Rules | News Rules | Blocked Senders |

Messages from senders in the list below will automatically be moved to the Deleted Items folder (for Mail messages) and/or not displayed (for Newsgroup messages).

Add Sender ×

Type the e-mail address (for example, someone@microsoft.com) or domain name (for example, microsoft.com) that you want to block.

Address: bill.sykes@newgate.com

Block the following:

    • Mail messages

    ○ News messages

    ○ Mail and News messages

OK   Cancel

Figure 9.1 *Blocking junk e-mail in Outlook Express*

couple of mouse clicks away from millions of pages of information, and the temptation is towards excessive searching, out of fear of missing some vital piece of information tucked away in the vast unruly collection. But resist the urge to seek information perfection. Nowhere does the 80:20 rule apply more than on the Internet (80 per cent of the results come from 20 per cent of the effort) and you can waste large amounts of time chasing a rapidly diminishing addition to useful data. Concentrate, instead, on precise and well-planned searches, as these will get you quickly to manageable quantities of quality information.

searching

Surfing – following links from one Web site to another – is the least effective way to locate specific information. You should start by adopting an appropriate search vehicle. An understanding of the different types will help you to choose the most appropriate for your needs.

Internet directories

Internet directories index sites under subject headings with progressively more specialized sub-headings. The most popular Internet directory is Yahoo (www.yahoo.co.uk). Approaching an information-gathering task via an Internet directory is rather like searching the catalogue of a library – fine for locating Web sites concerned with the subject you are interested in, but of limited value if what you are after is a specific reference which may be buried within a Web page. For that you need to use a search engine.

Search engines

Unlike directories, which are compiled by human beings, search engines are compiled and updated using 'Web crawling' software which trawls the World Wide Web looking for new pages and referencing the page contents. This leads to much greater volumes of information and the ability to pull out a reference from deep within a Web page. Locating the information you want is a matter of choosing the best combination of keywords. Two of the most popular search engines are AltaVista (www.altavista.co.uk), and Google (www.google.com).

There is increasing integration between Internet directories and search engines. Excite (www.excite.co.uk), Lycos (www. lycos.co.uk) and Infoseek (www.infoseek.com) now combine a search engine and directory. Note that a number of directories and search engines have UK Web addresses (those that end with 'co.uk') as well as the main North American address (ending in 'com'). This allows for more precise searching of specific UK data. The option to search the whole of the Web is still available. Some search engines, AltaVista for example, will search newsgroups as well as the World Wide Web.

metasearch tools

These send the same enquiry to a variety of search engines, and are useful if you are looking for a hard to find reference. Examples are the quaintly named Dogpile (www.dogpile.com) and Go2net (www.go2net.com).

searching tips

- ▓ Take care in formulating your search request. If you enter keywords that are too general, you risk being deluged with thousands of pages of information. Search engines rank response to queries, with those that most nearly meet the search criteria at the top of the list, but a vague enquiry may throw up hundreds of responses with similar rankings. Some lateral thinking may be necessary in choosing keywords likely to be in the material you are seeking.

- ▓ Use inverted commas to enclose phrases when you wish the search engine to look for the complete phrase rather than the individual words that comprise it. For example, entering the words *short extra cover* will throw up literally millions of references on everything from insurance to mattresses. Putting the same words in inverted commas produces about 50 references – all to do with cricket (short extra cover is a cricket field position). Use capital letters if you are looking for proper names – people, places or companies.

- ▓ Use optional 'operators' to narrow your search. All search engines employ devices for more sophisticated searching. Most use the '+' symbol to indicate words that must be included in the search results and the '–' symbol for any word that you specifically want to exclude. Using the keywords hotels *+Perth and –Scotland* will find hotels in Perth, Western Australia but will fitter out those in the Scottish town of the same name. Normally the use of plus and minus will be sufficient to target your search, but you can opt for more advanced searching with the Boolean operators (AND, OR, NOT, NEAR). Use of these varies slightly from one search engine to another, so for precise instructions on advanced searching, or if you have not encountered Boolean operators before, consult the help section of the search engine you are using.

■ Don't let yourself be distracted by links to other interesting but irrelevant pages. If something attracts your interest, use the bookmark or 'Favorites' facility to store a record of the location so that you can return to it at a later date.

■ Experiment with different search engines. Some are better than others for particular types of information. When you light upon one you like, make yourself familiar with its search conventions by looking up 'search tips' in its help menu. Then use it as your regular first-choice search vehicle.

■ Research has shown that even the best search engines are able to cover only a limited proportion of the World Wide Web (in a 1999 study, the highest proportion was estimated at 38 per cent). If, despite careful definition of your search words, your first-choice search engine fails to deliver the information you are looking for, try a different one or use a metasearch tool. You may get a better result.

revisiting useful sites

The 'Favorites' facility in Internet Explorer allows you to keep a note of interesting and useful sites you may have visited. The keyboard shortcut CTRL + D will add the current site to your Favorites list. To revisit the site at a later date, just click on the Favorites menu on your browser and select the site you want from the displayed list. If you are using Netscape Navigator as your browser, the same facility is known as 'Bookmarks'. Over time your Favorites list can become unwieldy unless you take the trouble to organize it. Set up folders for subject groups within the Favorites list and drop each new favourite site into the appropriate folder. When you click on a folder it will open up to display its contents. It is a good idea to prune your list from time to time of any favourite sites that have become redundant.

assessing quality

Finding information quickly is all very well, but what about the quality and reliability of what you discover? Within the estimated 800 million pages of information on the World Wide Web there is an awful lot of garbage. Anybody who wishes can quite simply set up a Web page and present information in an apparently authoritative way. So how do you discriminate between the reliable and the less so? Here are some pointers that may help:

■ *Is the site the work of a reputable body?* Generally at the top of the list for reliability are: universities; national government information sites; local authorities; publicly funded bodies; known voluntary organizations; reputable companies; broadcasters; online versions of respected newspapers and periodicals.

■ *Has the site been vetted in any way?* There are some sites and directories that make a positive commitment to verifying the quality of the links they carry. One such is About (www.about.com). Each of the categories in its directory is controlled by a specialist in the subject matter concerned.

■ *Is there anything else I can look for?* If a search comes up with information held on a Web site with which you are unfamiliar, you may get some clues regarding its reliability by considering the following:

- Are references given for any facts and figures, research or survey results?
- How up-to-date is the information? Normally the Web page will show a 'last reviewed' date.
- Does the information have a clear target audience and obvious purpose?
- What is the presentation like? While it may seem unfair to dismiss material on this basis, a slap-happy approach to spelling, grammar or presentation may indicate a similar attitude towards the veracity of information.
- Are there any clues to the status and expertise of the originator?
- Does the site contain links to other clearly reputable Web sites?

■ *Am I able to double-check the information?* Similar information on different Web sites may offer some guide to validity, but take care. Identical or near identical wording may indicate that it has simply been lifted from one site to the other.

getting a better turn of speed out of the Internet

For all the wonders of Internet technology, you can spend a lot of time twiddling your thumbs while you wait for the information you are after. Good search techniques will produce the greatest Internet time efficiencies, but there are a number of other things you can do to cut down wasted time:

■ *Select the best time of day to use the Internet.* As with any highway, increased traffic volume can mean an alarming reduction in speed. For European users, access to any US-based sites tends to be much faster in the morning while the bulk of their users are still asleep. Of course, if you are responsible for phone connection charges to your Internet service provider, you have to balance any time savings against increased phone charges.

▓ *Change your home page.* If your most common action on logging onto the Internet is to use a search engine, then make that search engine your home page. To change your home page if you are using Internet Explorer go to the Edit Menu and choose 'Internet Options'. With the General tab selected, type in the name of the site that you wish to be your new home page and click OK.

▓ *Turn off pictures.* These require much larger files than straight text, and will slow down your movement around the Internet considerably. You can switch them off in Internet Explorer by going into the Tools Menu, choosing the Advanced Option and then going to the multimedia section of the display. There is a downside. You may find navigating your way around a site more cumbersome as pictures are used extensively as links on which to click. However, you are always able to display a picture by right-clicking on the icon and choosing 'Show Picture' from the options, which are then displayed.

▓ *Make use of keyboard shortcuts.* There are a number of keyboard shortcuts that can save time on repetitive tasks. You will find a full list in the browser help file, but three useful examples are:
  – CTRL + F to access the find facility when you are looking for a particular piece of information on a Web page;
  – CTRL + ENTER when you are typing a Web page address. This will automatically put the prefix www. and the suffix .com into the address;

- CTRL + C to access the copy facility if you have selected some information in a Web page which you wish to copy into another document.

■ *Increase the cache size on your browser.* This is a location where pages that you have visited recently are stored so that, if they are accessed again, they can be loaded from your hard disk at greater speed than would be the case if they were accessed from the Internet. Provided you have plenty of disk space, you can set aside a larger proportion of your disk's capacity for this purpose. Users of Internet Explorer should select 'Options' within the Tools Menu, then click on 'Settings' to reveal a slider which will adjust the amount of disk space given over to temporary Internet files.

■ *Get a Web Accelerator.* There are a number of these available from software suppliers or download from the Internet. They work by anticipating your next move and downloading links in case you should click on them.

if you are responsible for your Internet connection

■ *Consider changing your Internet service provider.* Some run consistently faster than others. In these days of free access and free trials, it's easy enough to shop around. Search engines may also run more slowly because of heavy traffic. Try an alternative if the one you are using appears to be affected.

■ *Invest in the fastest available modem and check that it is set to run at its maximum speed.* Currently the standard modem will operate at up to 56 kilobytes per second. If you are still using a slower modem you can expect significant improvements by changing it.

However, don't expect a faster modem to solve delays that are the result of heavy Internet traffic. When you are stuck in a traffic jam it doesn't matter whether you are driving a Ferrari or a Ford Fiesta.

▓ *Investigate the possibility of higher speed access to the Internet.* The speed at which data can move between your computer and the Internet Access Point is limited by the nature of your telephone connection. High-speed access is a matter of increased bandwidth – turning a country lane into a motorway. High-speed connections are becoming more affordable as telephone companies reduce their charges. Contact your Internet Service Provider for current prices.

summary

Getting the best out of your use of the Internet is a matter of:

▓ dealing with incoming e-mail messages systematically and ensuring that they do not interrupt other work;

▓ maintaining clarity and economy in the e-mail messages you send;

▓ taking steps to prevent junk e-mail;

▓ adopting precise search techniques when seeking information on the Internet;

▓ monitoring the quality of information obtained;

▓ ensuring that your Internet connection is as efficient as possible.

organize yourself away from the office

Business trips and conferences can put a large spanner in your personal organization works. In the hours prior to your departure, you find yourself scurrying around to complete tasks that won't wait until your return. You finally manage to get away, drained and ratty, only to discover when you get to your destination that you have left a vital piece of information behind. In the course of your trip you are pestered by calls from the office which relate to a minor crisis, resolution of which is dependent on a piece of information that lurks somewhere in your filing system. Finally, you arrive back, exhausted, burdened with new work and facing a backlog of correspondence, voicemail and e-mail messages.

The key to retaining your equilibrium, when work takes you away from the office for days at a time, is good planning and adherence, wherever possible, to normal routines.

planning

- Build some space into your schedule, and scale back on any non-urgent work in the couple of days prior to your departure so that you can concentrate on those tasks that have to be completed before your return. Always allow more time for this than you think you will need.

▓ Cover your home base. Ensure that you have somebody who can check your mail, handle any minor crises, and find their way around your filing system and the information on your computer. Make sure you leave accurate contact numbers.

▓ Check and double-check that you have everything you need for the trip, but don't be tempted to take lots of paperwork in the vain hope that you will find time to deal with it. You are bound to come back with more than you took.

▓ Put together an 'out of office kit' comprising day-to-day accessories – envelopes, mini-stapler, pens, calculator, etc. Keep this handy so you can just drop it into your briefcase when you have a trip to make.

▓ If you have a number of locations to visit, plan the order to minimize travelling time. Journey-planning computer software may be of assistance in this.

▓ Make sure that you know how to carry out any unfamiliar tasks such as picking up your voicemail messages remotely, picking up e-mail, sending faxes from your portable computer, or tapping into your organization's network while on the road. Don't just trust to instructions from somebody else. Check the operation for yourself before you leave, to ensure it works. There is nothing worse than assuming that you will be able to stay in touch and then finding that you can't.

▓ Most importantly, make sure that you have any passwords you need to access the above-mentioned facilities.

▓ Change your voicemail message so that callers know you are away and when you will be back. Include a mobile number if appropriate. Remember to re-record your message when you return.

▓ Check that you have everything you need installed on your laptop computer – all relevant software, reference and contact material. The capacity and connectivity of today's portable computers means that you should be able to accommodate the same level of information as exists on your desktop PC. Keep data easily synchronized between laptop and desktop by using the 'briefcase' facility from Windows or another synchronization application.

▓ If you are using public transport, earmark some tasks that are particularly appropriate for completion while travelling. Normally this will mean tasks that are not reliant on major paper shuffling, and can put up with some degree of interruption.

▓ Don't underestimate the debilitating effect of travel. Allow some breathing space in your schedule before pitching into meetings and appointments.

▓ If your trip involves foreign travel, check that you have the correct adapters to connect your modem to the telephone system in the countries to which you are travelling. Suppliers such as Teleadapt (www. teleadapt.com) can provide adapters for any country. Make sure also that you know how to register your mobile phone to receive calls in the country or countries you are visiting.

▓ Some Internet service providers offer overseas Internet access at local call rates. If this is not available to you, or if you won't have a computer with you while you are abroad, you might like to consider setting up a free Web-based e-mail address, with a major site such as Yahoo (www.yahoo.com) or Hotmail (www.hotmail. com) These will allow you to send and receive mail from any Internet connected computer.

maintaining routines

■ Resist the temptation to bundle up conference papers, 'to be sorted out when I get back'. They will be destined to remain a disorganized bundle. Deal with any paperwork you receive while on the road in the same way as you would in the office (use the five Ds) and be particularly energetic with the 'discard' category.

■ Try to set some time aside during your day for dealing with routine correspondence and messages. When you tap into your e-mail and voicemail, deal with as much of it as possible, rather than just scanning through for major problem messages. This way, you will greatly ease the backlog of work waiting for you on your return.

■ Set up a working area in your hotel room that is as conducive to productivity as possible.

■ Keep track of expenses as you go. It's much easier than trying to remember them afterwards.

■ Give yourself a break. On conferences and business trips you can find yourself talking shop from breakfast until late night drinks in the bar. Build in some rest and relaxation if you don't want to return frazzled and exhausted.

■ Plan your first day back in the office before you return, but don't try to fit in too much.

summary

The biggest difficulties when working away from your normal base are the absence of facilities you usually take for granted and the disruption to your normal way of working. Deal with the first by good planning, and the second by maintaining routines as far as possible while you are away.

keep up the good work

We are all familiar with the phenomenon of resolution fatigue. Good intentions launched with enthusiasm and vigour on 31 December are abandoned and forgotten by 10 January. It's no different with decisions to improve personal organization. Reading this book is a start, but it won't bring all the results you want without some effort on your part.

set some targets

If you have not already done so, you should consider setting some goals in respect of your development of organizational skills. Look at the list below and prioritize items A, B or C according to their importance in lifting your current level of personal organization. The priority A items are the ones to concentrate on first. Set yourself an action plan for them, complete with dates by which you will review progress. Don't take on too much on at once. Remember that you need to give new habits time to become established.

Aim	Priority
establish greater overall direction in my work	_____
improve objective setting and prioritizing skills	_____
use effective time planning and tracking tools	_____
meet deadlines	_____
schedule tasks at appropriate times	_____
overcome procrastination	_____
develop new work habits	_____
sharpen up decision making	_____
adopt a systematic approach to incoming paper	_____
combat paper overload	_____
read more efficiently	_____
improve memory	_____
handle meetings effectively	_____
delegate more	_____
overcome distractions and interruptions	_____
help others to be more organized	_____
learn to say no	_____
organize office space	_____
manage desk space	_____
organize filing systems	_____
prune and weed files	_____
organize computer files	_____
use information technology more fully	_____
acquire and learn new software packages	_____
manage e-mail and voicemail effectively	_____
get the best out of the Internet	_____
organize myself away from the office	_____

review progress

Keep your priority A action plan handy. Review progress initially monthly and then three-monthly. Give yourself immediate positive reinforcement or reward for every step forward, and use your successes as stepping stones to further achievement. Be kind with yourself when you have failed to achieve the progress you anticipated. Look for the reasons: perhaps you were trying to achieve too many things at once, maybe you didn't bash away for long enough to establish a new habit. Don't let yourself be lured into abandoning your goals, however. Reframe them and move on.

Visualize the way that you will work and the benefits that will accrue when you have perfected the new skills and ways of working. Visualization is a very powerful means of seeing you through the short-term pain and into the long-term gain. Once your priority A goals are well underway, you can move on to priority B.

remaining on track in the face of job changes

A change of job is bound to cause some disruption to your personal organization. The secret to minimizing this is to distinguish between those aspects of the way you work which will be unaffected by a change of environment and those where you may need to engage in some reflection and adaptation. Your approach to such things as scheduling your time, dealing with paper, and using technology are unlikely to require any adjustment. It is in the field of people relationships and your attitude towards inherited systems and priorities that you may need to adjust.

taking over somebody else's system and priorities

When you arrive in a new job fired up for the challenge, there is a natural inclination to shape it to your way of working. Fine, every reason why you should, but don't assume that the way you have done things in the past is the only way, and will work in all situations. A lot of energy can be wasted and good ideas lost when new incumbents fail to take enough time to understand what they have inherited before they start hacking and burning. The previous person who did your job may have adopted a particular way of working in response to circumstances that may not immediately be apparent. So before you reorder priorities and restructure systems, ask why they were done that way.

working with new people

The person you will be most conscious of adjusting to is your new boss. In the absence of clear indications to the contrary, it's easy to make the mistake of assuming that he or she will behave in the same way as your previous boss. And remember, your new boss may be making similar wrong assumptions about you. If your boss doesn't raise the matter, suggest a discussion on the way in which you will work together, but first give yourself a few days to find your feet, so that you are in a position to know what you are talking about. If you are a member of an established team, you can sound out other members before embarking on this conversation.

The way you approach your new job will also have an impact on junior colleagues. New ways of working – increased delegation, changes to meetings etc – may enthuse or arouse deep antagonism depending on how they are presented. So, once again, take time to understand why things have been done in a particular way before introducing changes. When you do so, take account of the following points:

- People will tend to focus on their own self-interest when changes are introduced – you need to sell the benefits.
- There is great scope for misunderstanding of motives, especially with a new manager who has yet to obtain people's trust, so ensure that you discuss proposals adequately and give people the opportunity to raise points.
- People are more likely to embrace change if they can feel that they have been involved in the process of diagnosis and decision.